Free

   Fun

      Unlimited

Play With Small BOXES

by

Liz & Dick Wilmes

Illustrations by
Carol Koeller

A **BUILDING BLOCKS** Publication

38W567 Brindlewood, Elgin, Illinois 60123

ART:

Cover and Text Illustrations:

Carol Koeller
Early Childhood Illustrator
Chicago, Illinois

Cover Design and Layout:

David VanDelinder
Studio 155
Elgin, Illinois

Text and Graphics Layout:

Karen Wollscheid
McHenry, Illinois

PUBLISHED BY:

38W567 Brindlewood
Elgin, Illinois 60123

ISBN 0-943452-24-4

DEDICATED TO

**ALL CHILDREN
WHO THINK
SMALL BOXES
ARE WONDERFUL
TO PLAY WITH.**

CONTENTS

Fingerplays

Language Activities

Active Games

Art

Learning Centers

FINGER PLAYS

DIAL "911" FOR SAFETY

Dial "911" for Safety

(tune: Here We Go Round the Mulberry Bush)

This is the way we dial for safety,
Dial for safety, dial for safety.
This is the way we dial for safety,
Dial 911 for safety.

by Dick Wilmes

Activity

Make very simple telephones for all the children out of quart milk bottle cartons. *(See illustration.)*

Sit with a small group of children/individual. Talk about different emergency situations that could happen at their homes. *What would they do? How would they call the operator for help?*

Give the children their telephones. Sing DIAL 911 FOR SAFETY. As they are singing, let them practice dialing "911." At the end of the song you be the operator at the police or fire station. Let the children take turns describing their emergencies. Encourage the children to tell their names and be clear about the emergency they are telling about.

FRIEND IN THE BOX

Friend In The Box

Friend in the box.
Friend in the box.
Who is that
Friend in the box?

Activity

Get a box that will comfortably fit over a child's head – maybe a 5 gallon ice cream container. Cut eyes, nose, and mouth openings in it.

Have the children sit in a circle so that they can see each other. Have them close their eyes or cover them with their hands. You walk around the outside of the group. Tap one child on the shoulder. Have him quietly walk to the center of the circle, sit down, and put the box over his head.

Have the children uncover their eyes and look at the child in the middle. Say the FRIEND IN THE BOX rhyme and guess who is hiding in the box. When the child in the middle hears his name, he should take off the box and stand up. Play again.

BOX OF APPLES

Box Of Apples

Box of apples, box of apples.
Who has it now?
Let's look around the group
And see who takes a bow.

Activity

Use the pattern and cut lots of red, yellow, and green felt apples. Put them in a small box.

Have everyone sit in a circle and put their hands behind their backs. As the children are saying BOX OF APPLES, have them pass the box behind them around the circle. The person holding the box at the end, takes a bow and puts an apple on the felt board. Keep playing until all the apples are on the felt board. Count them. Count the red ones – the yellow ones – the green ones. *(Could have apple wedges for snack.)*

RAKE THE LEAVES

Rake The Leaves

Leaves, leaves
   (Arms wave.)

Big and small
   (Hands and arms apart – Hands close.)

See if we can rake them all.
   (Raking motion.)

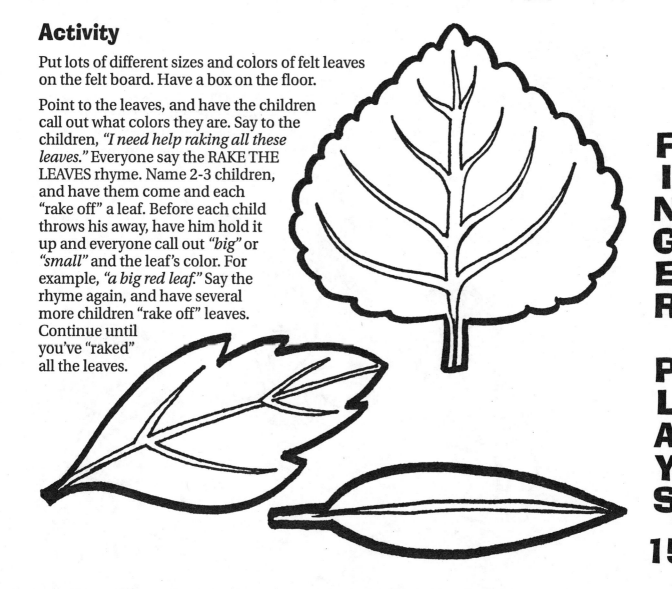

Activity

Put lots of different sizes and colors of felt leaves on the felt board. Have a box on the floor.

Point to the leaves, and have the children call out what colors they are. Say to the children, *"I need help raking all these leaves."* Everyone say the RAKE THE LEAVES rhyme. Name 2-3 children, and have them come and each "rake off" a leaf. Before each child throws his away, have him hold it up and everyone call out *"big"* or *"small"* and the leaf's color. For example, *"a big red leaf."* Say the rhyme again, and have several more children "rake off" leaves. Continue until you've "raked" all the leaves.

LET'S BE FIREFIGHTERS

Let's Be Firefighters

(tune: 1 Little, 2 Little, 3 Little Children)

Hurry, hurry drive the fire truck. (Drive.)
Hurry, hurry drive the fire truck.
Hurry, hurry drive the fire truck.
Early in the morning.

Hurry, hurry turn the corner… (Turn wheel.)
Hurry, hurry find the fire… (Look around.)
Hurry, hurry climb the ladder… (Hand over hand.)
Hurry, hurry spray the water… (Hold fire hose.)
Hurry, hurry back to the station… (Drive slowly.)

by Mary Schuring and Cheryl Luppino

Activity

Have a red plate steering wheel for each child. Pass them out. Let the children drive their fire trucks as they sing, LET'S BE FIREFIGHTERS. When they get to the fire, remind them to get out of the trucks *(put down the steering wheels)* and put out the fire. Get back in *(pick up the steering wheels)* and drive back.

OLD MOTHER HUBBARD'S CUPBOARD

Old Mother Hubbard

Old Mother Hubbard went to the cupboard
   (Walk arms.)

To get her poor dog a bone.

When she got there, the cupboard was bare,
   (Open cupboard.)

And her poor little dog had none.
   (Shake head "no.")

Make OLD MOTHER HUBBARD'S CUPBOARD

Have a medium size box representing Old Mother Hubbard's cupboard. *(Optional: Cover the box with patterned adhesive paper.)* Stand it on the floor, so the opening is facing the children.

Activity

Say OLD MOTHER HUBBARD with the children. Then say something like, *"Oh no! There is nothing in Mother Hubbard's cupboard. Let's go to the grocery store and buy food for her."*

bananas
dog biscuits
apples
milk
beans

Have a clipboard, paper and pencil. Have the children use their hands to take a pretend walk to the store. When they arrive, have the children get a cart. Have them go around the store "buying" food they think Mother Hubbard and her dog would like. Write down all the items as the children call them out.

Walk back home. After they're back, have them try to remember all the foods that they bought. As the children name the foods, have them come up and pretend to put the foods in the cupboard. Check the foods off the list as they are named. If there are any foods left on the list, read them, and have the children put them into the cupboard.

BUYING A DONUT

Bakery

Down around the corner
In the bakery shop,
There were lots of little doughnuts
With sugar on top.
Along came (child's name) *all alone.*
She bought a (color) *one and ran on home.*

Activity

Cut different colored poster board doughnuts. Put them in a bakery box. Set the box of doughnuts in the middle of the group.

Chant the BAKERY rhyme. Each time you say it, name a child, let her skip, walk, etc. to the bakery box and pick her "favorite" doughnut. Name the color she chose in the last line. Continue until all the children have had their fill of doughnuts. Have a pretend snack. *"How were your doughnuts?"*

BIRTHDAY GIFTS

Gift Boxes

Gift boxes, gift boxes, everywhere.
  (Wave hands.)

Empty now, they're lighter than air.

Some tiny as bugs, one big as a bear.
  (Hands together – Hands apart.)

Round, rectangular, even square.
  (Make shapes with hands.)

by Vohny Moehling

Make a GIFT BOX

Wrap a medium size gift box with plain paper. Write the GIFT BOXES rhyme on one side of the box. Have several different colored wide markers.

Activity

Sit on the floor with the children. Set the box in front of you. Read the rhyme to them. Tell the children to pretend that it is their birthday. What gifts would they like to receive? Let each child choose what color marker he'd like and then you write his BIRTHDAY GIFT on the box.

Put the decorated gift box in housekeeping. Have lots of birthday parties and other celebrations.

FINGER PLAYS

19

TOY BOX

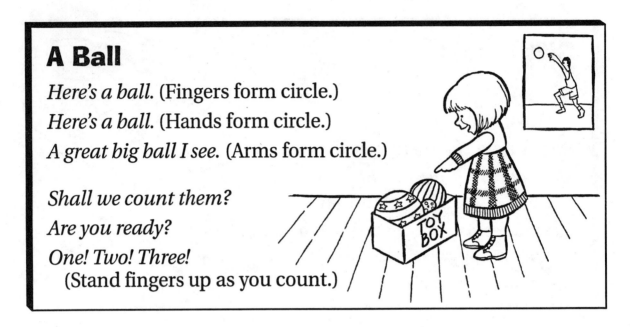

A Ball

Here's a ball. (Fingers form circle.)

Here's a ball. (Hands form circle.)

A great big ball I see. (Arms form circle.)

Shall we count them?

Are you ready?

One! Two! Three!
   (Stand fingers up as you count.)

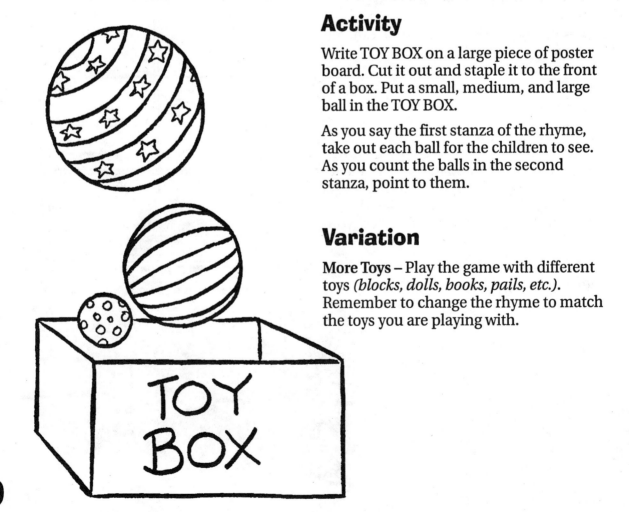

Activity

Write TOY BOX on a large piece of poster board. Cut it out and staple it to the front of a box. Put a small, medium, and large ball in the TOY BOX.

As you say the first stanza of the rhyme, take out each ball for the children to see. As you count the balls in the second stanza, point to them.

Variation

More Toys – Play the game with different toys *(blocks, dolls, books, pails, etc.)*. Remember to change the rhyme to match the toys you are playing with.

TING-A-LING

Ting-A-Ling

You are a circus clown
Your name is Ting-A-Ling.
You do a funny trick
Inside your circus ring.

Activity

Put a large shallow box or box top in the middle of the group area.

Have a child or pair of children be Ting-A-Ling, and stand in the middle of their circus ring *(box)*. As the other children say the TING-A-LING rhyme, the "circus clown/s" in the middle does her trick. Everybody clap. Let other child/ren be Ting-A-Lings, and play again and again.

JACK/JILL-IN-THE-BOX

Jack/Jill-In-The-Box

Jack-in-the-box (Crouch down.)
Jack-in-the-box

Will you come out?
Yes, he will! (Pop out.)
 Or
No, he won't! (Stay down.)

Make SEVERAL POP UP PUPPETS

for each one:

1. Duplicate the 2 puppet patterns.

2. Color them. Glue them back-to-back with a popsicle stick in the middle.

3. Cut a slit in the bottom of a juice box.

4. Cut top off the top of the juice box.

5. Slip the puppet into the slit so s/he pops up through the top.

Activity

Bring the puppets to group time. Give each one to a child. Everyone say JACK/JILL-IN-THE-BOX. At the last line, each child who has a puppet calls out what he wants his puppet to do and works the puppet to do it. Everyone claps. Give other children the puppets and play again.

Extension

More Puppet Play – Put the puppets in the language area for children to use during free choice.

FINGER PLAYS

23

MAIL A LETTER

Letters, Letters

Letters, letters

Red, white, and blue.
(Hold up 3 fingers.)

I'll write a nice one
(Pretend writing.)

And mail it to you.
(Give letter to friend next to you.)

Make a SIMPLE MAILBOX

Get a medium size box and paint it blue. Cut a wide slit in the top. Using white and/or red paint, print "MAIL" on the sides of the box.

Activity

Put the "Mailbox" and a basket of red and blue crayons in the middle of a table. Have white paper. Say LETTERS, LETTERS with the children. Give each child paper. Let them use the crayons to write/draw letters and then mail them.

Extension

Letter Writing – Duplicate the LETTERS, LETTERS rhyme. Glue it on a small piece of poster board. Hang it on a wall in the writing area. Put the crayons, paper, and "Mailbox" on the writing table. Let the children write/draw lots of letters and mail them to each other.

SIGNS OF SPRING

Hibernation   by Vohny Moehling

Deep underground I'll make my nest, (Cover head with arms.)

All curled up for a nice long rest.

Don't wake me for anything, (Shake head "no.")

Until you see the first signs of spring.
   (Walk around group showing big sun to everyone. Each animal wakes up.)

Make Your SPRING PICTURES

Have different magazine pictures depicting the signs of spring. Get several medium size boxes that the children can easily curl up and hibernate in. Cut the tops off. Set them in the middle of your group area.

Activity

Have children curl up in the boxes and pretend to be hibernating animals in their winter homes. Say HIBERNATION with the other children. As you say the last line, show one spring picture to each "animal." When he sees it, he wakes up, calls out what it is, and climbs out of his winter home. When all the animals have woken up, clap for them. Play again.

WHERE ARE THE ANTS?

Ant Hill

Once I saw an ant hill (Make fist.)
With no ants about.
So I asked, "Dear little ants, (Talk to "ants" in fist.)
Won't you please come out?"

Then, as if the little ants
Had heard my call.
One, two, three, four, five came out!
    (Hold up fingers.)
And that was all. (Shrug shoulders.)

Make an ANT HILL

Get a tiny brown box with a lid to use for the ant hill. Duplicate the strip of 5 ants. *(Color if you'd like.)* Roll up the strip and put it in the box, so the beginning of the strip just peeks out the top when covered.

Activity

Set the ant hill on the floor. Say ANT HILL with the children. Slowly count the ants as you pull them out of the "hill."

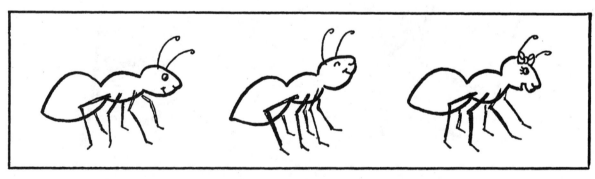

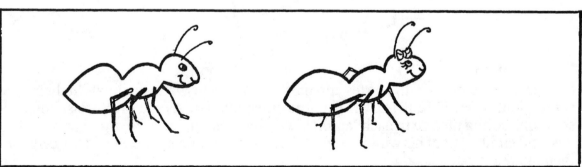

1-2-3 ANTS

1, 2, 3 Ants

(adapted from traditional rhyme)

1, 2, 3 (Hold up fingers.)
There's an ant on me.

Where did he go? (Look around.)
I don't know. (Shrug shoulders.)

Activity

Duplicate the ant pattern. Say 1, 2, 3 ANTS with the children. As you are saying it, place the ant someplace on your body *(on your foot, on top of your head, under your arm, between your fingers, etc.)*. After the rhyme say to the children, *"Oh yes you do! Look around and find the ant on my body."* Have the children look around and call out where it is. Play again and again.

After several times, give the ant to a child and let her put it on her body. Keep changing children and repeating the rhyme.

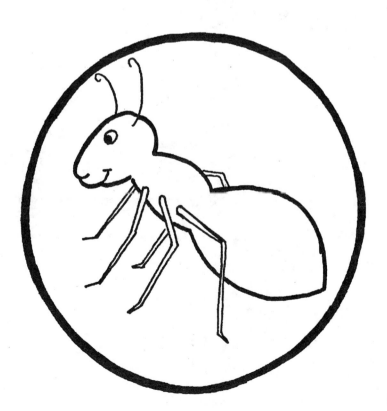

PLANTING TIME

Planting
by Dick Wilmes

I took a little seed one day
About a month ago.
I put it in a pot of dirt
In hopes that it would grow.

I poured a little water,
To make the soil right.
I set the pot upon the sill,
Where the sun would give it light.

I checked the pot most every day,
And turned it once or twice.
With a little care and water,
I helped it grow so nice.

Activity

Set up a flower planting area in a sunny area of your room. Duplicate the PLANTING rhyme. Back it on a small piece of poster board and hang it at eye level near the planting activity.

Let the children plant seeds in small milk cartons and/or other plasticized boxes such as cottage cheese, yogurt or spreadable cheese. Put them in the sun and care for them each day.

28

PLANTING

I took a little seed one day
About a month ago.

I put it in a pot of dirt
In hopes that it would grow.

I poured a little water,
To make the soil right.

I set the pot upon the sill,
Where the sun would give it light.

I checked the pot most every day,
And turned it once or twice.

With a little care and water,
I helped it grow so nice.

by Dick Wilmes

Building Blocks
38W567 Brindlewood, Elgin, Illinois 60123

WHERE ARE THE BEES?

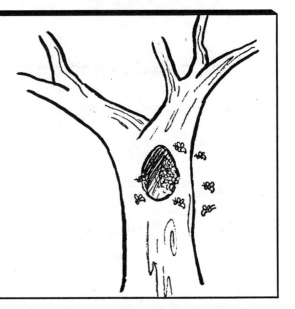

Where Are The Bees?

Here is the beehive. (Make fist.)
Where are the bees? (Look at fist.)
Hidden away where nobody sees.

Here they come creeping
Out of the hive.
1, 2, 3, 4, 5. (Stand up fingers.)

Make a QUICK BEEHIVE

Duplicate 5 bees. *(Color if you want.)*
Get a small box with a lid to use for the
beehive. Cut a long slit in each side and
the top. Slip one bee in each slit, so it
barely comes through to the outside.

Activity

Bring the beehive full of bees to group
time. Say WHERE ARE THE BEES with
the children. Slowly count at the end.
Let the children pull out the bees, and
fly them around and back to the hive.
Put them in the hive and play again.

POTATO GARDENS

Growing In The Sun

*The sun comes up
with a great big smile,*

*And shines on the
ground for awhile.*

*It warms up the
vegetables planted below,*

*And helps them to
grow and grow and grow.*

by Dick Wilmes

Activity

Cut down small dairy boxes for the children. Have a potato for each child. Let each child help you cut off the top and bottom of his potato. Place one potato in each dairy box. Scoop out some of each potato. Plant mustard seeds in the cavity. Gently water and set in a sunny window. Take care of them daily. Watch them grow.

Extension

Growing In the Sun – Duplicate GROWING IN THE SUN for each child. Glue it on a popsicle stick. Stick the rhyme in each vegetable pot.

I STUCK MY HEAD IN A LITTLE SKUNK'S HOLE

I Stuck My Head In A Little Skunk's Hole

I stuck my head in a little skunk's hole,
And the little skunk said, "Why bless my soul.
Take it out, take it out, take it out.
Remove it."

I didn't take it out and the little skunk said,
"You better take it out or you'll wish you had.
Take it out, take it out, take it out."
Shh-h-h-h-h-h, I removed it too late.

Make SKUNK HOLES

Duplicate the skunk pattern 5-6 times. *(Color if you want.)* Glue the skunks to the insides of the shoe boxes. Bring them to group time.

Activity

Ask the children, *"Who wants to stick his head in a skunk's hole?"* Give each child who wants, a box. Say the rhyme. As you say the first line let the children stick their heads in the skunks' holes. At the end, everyone hold his nose, while the children come out of the skunks' holes.

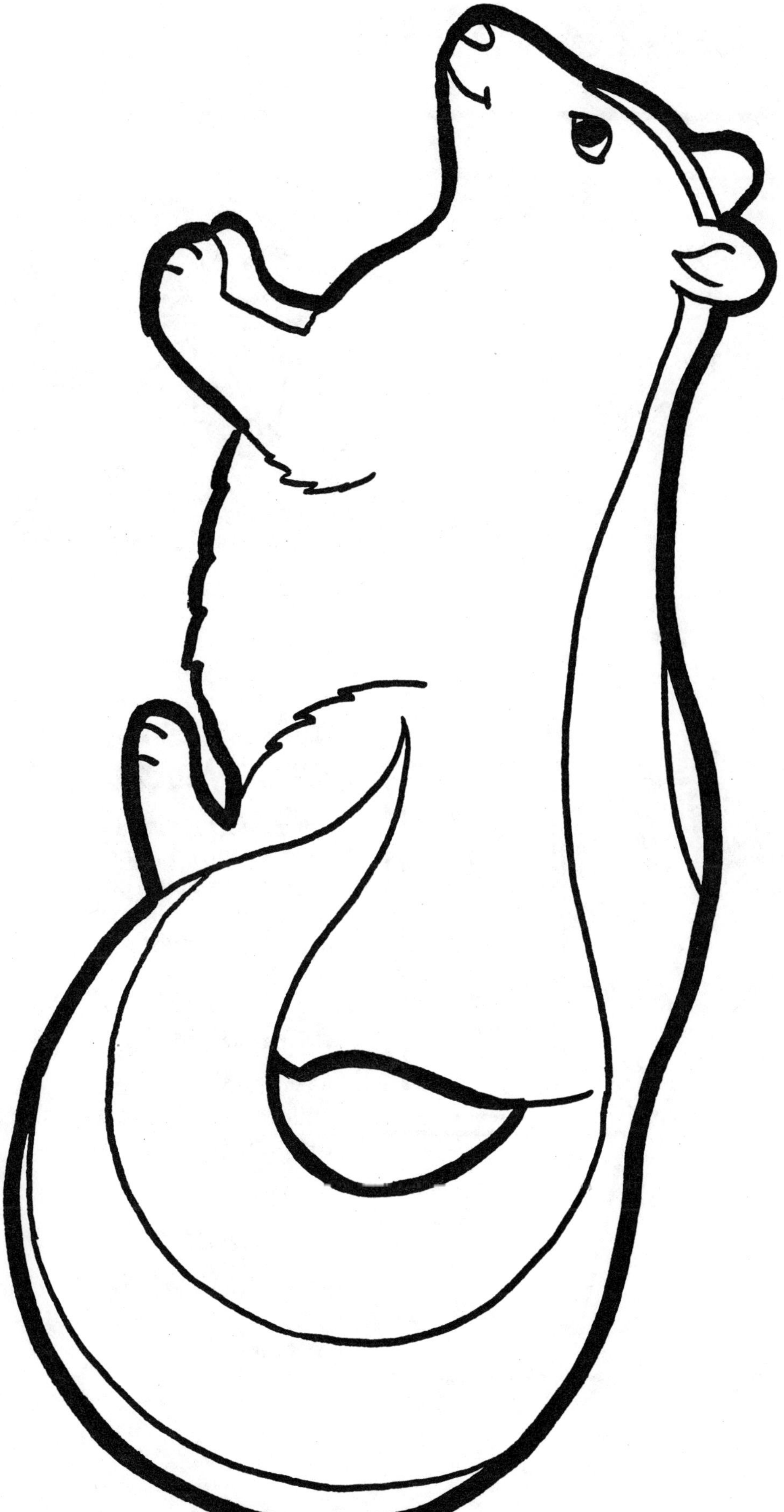

RED SAYS STOP

Red Says Stop

Red says STOP.
Green says GO.
Yellow says WAIT.
Be sure you know!

Make a Simple STOP AND GO LIGHT

Get a quart size milk carton. Cover it with yellow paper. Cut out red, yellow, and green construction paper circles. Glue them to the box to make the light.

Activity

As you say the rhyme with the children, point to each color on the light.

Extension

Block Play – Put the LIGHT in the block area. You may want to make several more.

COOKIE JAR

Who Ate The Cookie From The Cookie Jar?

Who ate a cookie from the cookie jar?

(Name) *ate a cookie from the cookie jar.*

Who me? (Child points to self.)

Yes, you. (Shake head "yes" while pointing at child.)

Couldn't be. (Child shakes head "no.")

Then who. (Look around for another child.)

Make a QUICK COOKIE JAR

Write COOKIE JAR on a piece of poster board. Staple it to the front of a large laundry detergent concentrate box.

Activity

Show the COOKIE JAR to the children. Turn it over to show them that there are no cookies in it. Look at all the children and say, *"I thought there were some cookies in the jar. I guess not. I wonder who ate them? Let's find out."* Say the rhyme with the children and then have some graham crackers for snack.

LANGUAGE ACTIVITIES

TELEPHONE

Activity

Give each child a quart milk box to use as a telephone. Put your telephone up to your ear and "call" the child next to you. She answers the phone. Whisper a message to her. She calls the child next to her. That child answers and listens to the message. Continue passing the message on for 3-4 children. The last person to hear the message says it aloud. Play again and again with new messages.

WAKE UP THE ANIMALS

Activity

Get a medium size box and 7-8 different stuffed animals. Set the animals on the floor for everyone to see. Point to each one and have the children tell what animal it is and then quietly say *"good night"* to him in his "language." As the children are whispering *"good night"* gently put the animals in the box bed. When all the animals are in bed, cover them with a blanket. Read a story to the children and animals.

TIME TO WAKE UP! Have the children name one of the sleeping animals. Peek under the blanket and pick up that animal. Have the children say *"hi – time to get up – good morning"* to that animal in his "language." Continue to wake up all the animals. If the children forget some of the animals, simply wake them yourself at the end.

Extension

Play With the Animals – Put the animals in the block area, so they can watch the children build and play.

NAME BOX

Make the NAME BOX

1. Get a paper gallon milk box. Wash it out and let dry. *(Optional: Cover with patterned adhesive paper.)*

2. Carefully cut a 2" slit in the box for each child in your room.

3. Cut a 2"x 6" posterboard card for each child. Write each child's name on a card.

4. Slip each name card into a slit in the milk box.

Activity

Bring the NAME BOX to the first group time of each day. Say to the children, *"Give a smile, give a cheer. Let us know that _____ is here."* As you do, pull out a name, hold the card for everyone to see, and read the name aloud. That child stands up and comes over to you as everyone claps for him. When he gets to you, give him a hug or high-5, and let him put his name card in a small basket on the floor. Repeat for each child.

Variation

Lead the Exercise – Put all the name cards in the NAME BOX. Have a child come up, pull a name out of the box, and give it to you. Read the name on the card. That child should stand up and lead the class in an exercise. *(If he needs encouragement, hold his hand and do the exercise with him.)*

FALL MEMORY

Activity

Have bark, leaves, acorns, pine cones, roots, seeds, twigs, flowers, fruit, etc. in a shallow box or box top. *(At least one item for each child.)*

Sit with the children. Hold up each item and let the children call out what it is. Pass the box around and let each child pick an item. As she picks it, she should hold it up for everyone to see and then put it behind her back. After all the items are hidden, say to the children, *"I'm looking for an acorn."* Everyone points to the child who's hiding it. If the child who everyone's pointing to has the 'acorn' she puts it in the box; if not she shakes her head *'no.'* The child who has the acorn brings it out, shows it, and puts it in the box.

FOOD BASKET

Activity

Get a large basket. Fill it with lots of food boxes and some non-food boxes.

Sit with the children, and talk about all the items they buy at the grocery store with their moms and dads. After talking, bring out the FOOD BASKET. Quickly take out each box, have the children call out what it is, and set it in front of you. Hold up each box again and ask, *"Is this a food box?"* If the answer is *"yes"* put it in the FOOD BASKET; if the answer is *"no,"* leave it on the floor.

Play Some More – Have the children cover their eyes. Stand 4-5 food related and one or more non-food related boxes in a row. Have the children uncover their eyes, look at all the boxes, and call out which one/s doesn't belong to the food group and why. Play again and again mixing different selections of boxes.

FOOD TRIANGLE

Enlarge the FOOD TRIANGLE, glue it to a piece of colored construction paper, and laminate or cover it with clear adhesive paper. Hang at the children's eye level. Talk about the different foods.

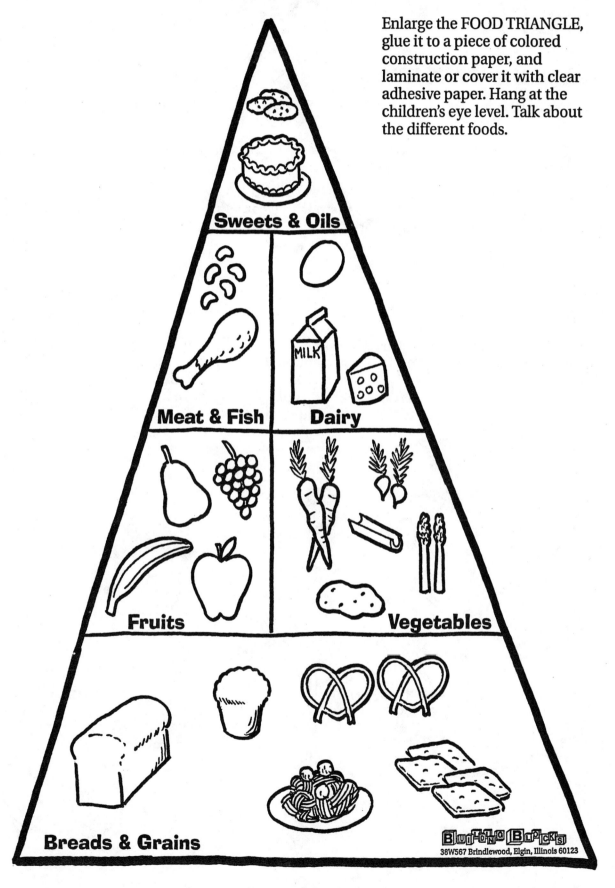

Sweets & Oils

Meat & Fish   Dairy

Fruits   Vegetables

Breads & Grains

LANGUAGE

FEED THE HUNGRY CLOWN

Make the HUNGRY CLOWN

1. Get a shoe box. Duplicate the HUNGRY CLOWN pattern. Glue it to the outside bottom side of the box.

2. Carefully cut out the clown's mouth. *(Remember safety.)* Put the top back on the box.

3. Find magazine/catalogue pictures of the 6 food groups. Cut them out, glue them to tagboard, and laminate or cover them with clear adhesive paper. Put the game cards in the box so they are ready to use when you want to play.

4. Put FEED THE HUNGRY CLOWN on a shelf so it is readily available.

Activity

Sit with the children. Have the HUNGRY CLOWN and the food pictures in front of you. Pass out all the food pictures. Have the children lay the pictures in front of them. Say, *"Bread is the food group we eat the most of. In the bread group is (name examples). Who has some bread for HUNGRY CLOWN?"* The children who have bread pictures should come up and feed him. As they do, they could name the bread. Continue with the other food groups.

HUNGRY CLOWN PATTERN

TOY BOX

Make the TOY BOX

1. Separately wrap the top and bottom of a medium size box.

2. Cut an opening in one side of the gift box, just large enough for a child to reach his hand into.

3. Put 5-6 different toys in the box. Cover it. *(If this is too difficult, let the children see the toys and then put them in the box.)*

Activity

Sit with a small group of children. Have the TOY BOX in front of you. Tell the children that the BOX is filled with different toys.

Name a child. Have her come up, put her hand into the box, and feel a toy. *"What does she think it could be?"* Have her continue to hold it. You slightly tip the box top open and take out the toy she has chosen. Hold it up for everyone to see and call out what it is. Continue until the TOY BOX is empty.

GIFT BOXES

Activity

Wrap several different sizes and shapes of boxes in a variety of wrapping paper. *(Wrap the tops and bottoms separately, but with matching paper.)* Gather 10-15 types of gifts that would fit in at least one of the boxes. Put these gifts in a big sack/ pillow case.

Sit with the children. Put the wrapped boxes in front of you. Pull out the first gift from the sack. Talk about what it is and who it could be for. Ask the children, *"Which box would this gift fit in the best?"* After they have decided, ask a child to put the gift in the box. Did it fit? Continue to play. *(If you have a gift that fits in an already filled box, take the first gift out and set it in front of the box.)*

PASS THE MITTENS

Activity

Collect pairs of mittens to equal at least half the children. Put the mittens in a box.

Sit in a circle with the children. Put on a record, and begin passing one mitten around the circle. Stop the music. Whoever has the mitten puts it on. Start the music again and pass the next mitten. Continue in this way until all the mittens have been passed.

Now have each child put his mittened hand/s in front of him. Point to a child. Have her hold up her mittened hand. Have the rest of the children look at their mittens. The mates come to the middle, shake hands, take off their mittens, and put them back in the box. Continue until all the mittens have been paired and are back in the box. *(Optional: Put the box of mittens in the language area for the children to play with during free choice.)*

MITTEN MATCH

Activity

Bring a shoe box to circle time. Have the children bring their mittens.

Each child should keep one mitten and put the mate in the shoe box. Now have the children pass the one mitten to the person next to him. Put on that mitten. Hold up one of the mittens in the box. Say, *"Look at the mitten you are wearing. If the one I'm holding matches the one you are wearing, come here and we'll make a pair."* Give the mate to the child and let him wear it for the rest of the game.

Continue until everyone is wearing a pair of mittens. Pass the box around the circle and have the children put one mitten back in it. After that, take off the second mitten and pass it to the person next to him. Now you're ready to play again.

WEATHER CUBE

Activity

Get a plastic photo box. Enlarge and color the 6 weather pictures – windy, snowy, rainy, stormy, cloudy, and sunny *(or use magazine pictures)*. Slip one picture into each side of the box.

At circle time roll the box to a child. Have him tell what type of weather is facing up on the box and what he likes to do in that type of weather *(or one type of clothes she wears)*. Have that child roll the WEATHER CUBE to another child. Continue in this manner.

Variation

More CONVERSATION CUBES

🔳 **Sky Cube** – stars, moon, sun, clouds, rainbow, lightning.

🔳 **Occupations Cube** – 6 workers children are most familiar with.

🔳 **Feelings Cube** – 6 faces which portray obvious emotions.

WEATHER PATTERNS ☞

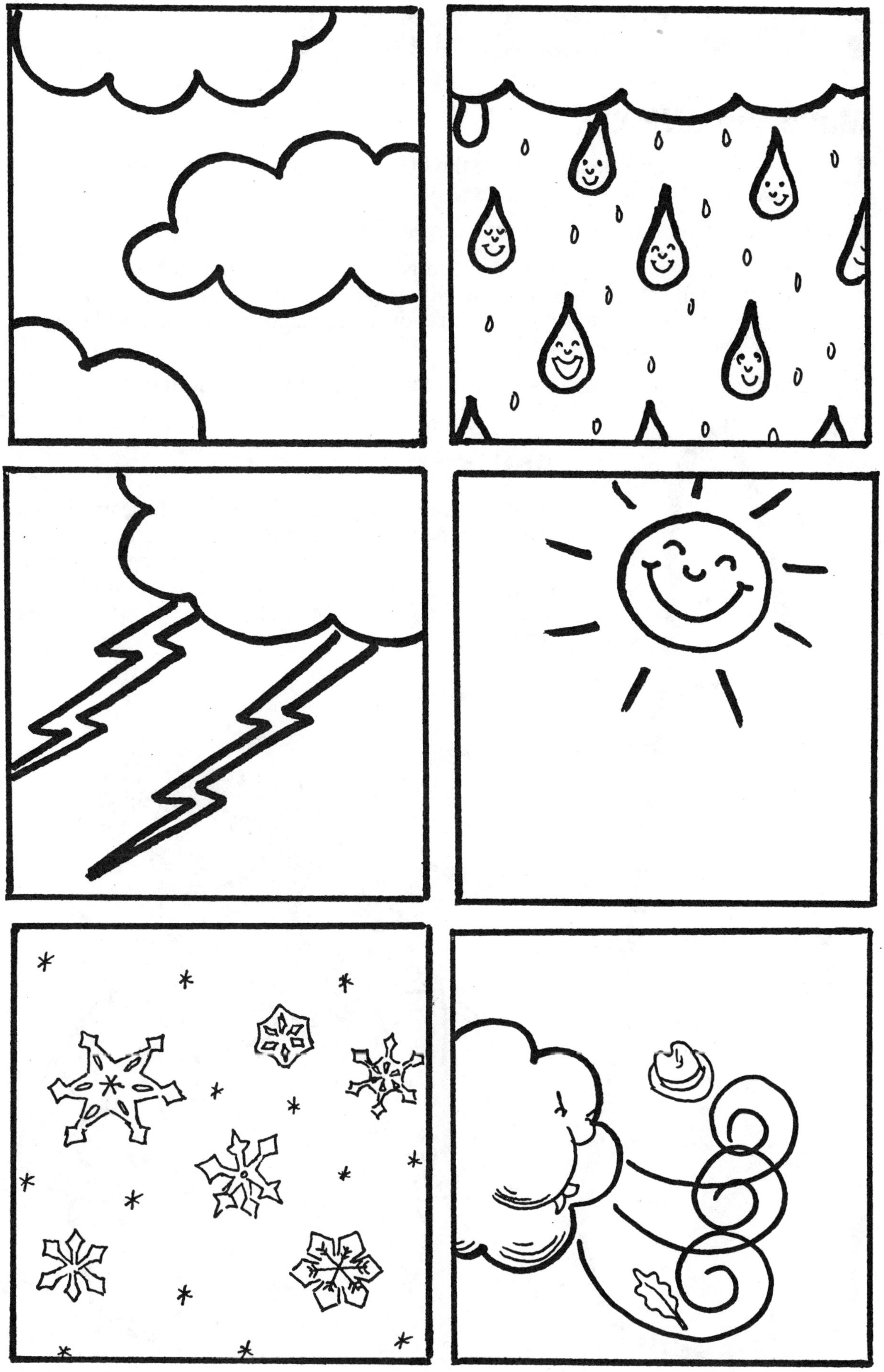

FEED THE BUNNY

Make the BUNNY

1. Get a half gallon milk box. Duplicate the BUNNY pattern. Glue it to the side of the box.

2. Carefully cut out the bunny's mouth. *(Remember safety.)*

3. Using the carrot pattern make lots of orange construction paper carrots. Pick a category that the children are familiar with *(shapes, letters, numbers, colors, foods, toys, animals, vehicles, etc.)*. Draw pictures or stick stickers on the carrots of things in that category.

4. Make different sets of carrots so you can feed the bunny different "foods."

Activity

Set the bunny on a chair. Pass out all of his carrots. Say, *"Let's feed the bunny some red carrots. Those who have a red sticker on their carrots come up and feed the bunny."* Continue with the rest of colors. Now the bunny is full, so he'll hop off to play with his friends. *"Bye! See you all again!"*

BUNNY PATTERN

PULL THE COLOR STRIP

Make the COLOR STRIP

1. Unroll about 2-3 feet of wide adding machine tape. With different colored markers, draw large dots along the strip. *(Leave about an inch between dots.)*

2. Roll up the tape and put it in a small box. Have the beginning edge of the roll peek out the top.

Activity

Sit with the children. Hold up the box. Pull the tape until the first colored dot appears. Have the children call out the color. Pass the box to a child. Have her pull the tape until the next dot appears. Let her hold it up and everyone call out the color. Pass the box again, let a child pull the color strip, and everyone call the new color. Continue until the children have pulled the whole color strip.

Variation

More Strips – Make additional strips and play in the same way. Use stickers or draw your own letters, numbers, and figures.

- Letters
- Numbers
- Animals
- Foods
- Toys

FLOWER BOX

Activity

Use the patterns and cut out lots of construction paper flowers. Glue each one to a popsicle stick. Fill a shoe box about half full of sand.

Gather the construction paper flowers into a bouquet. Put the box of sand in the middle of the group. Plant your flower garden. Say, *"Carol, pick the red flower from the bouquet and plant it in our FLOWER BOX."* Child does. Name another child and let him plant a flower. Continue until the FLOWER BOX is completely planted.

Hint – To keep more children continually involved, name 2 or 3 children at a time to plant the flowers.

FLOWER
PATTERNS

NAME THAT COLOR

Activity

Get a shoe box. Cut a 3" opening in one end. Gather 10-15 different solid color scarves and tie them together into one long streamer. Put the steamer in the box with the first scarf just peeking out of the opening.

Hand the box to a child. Have him slowly pull the scarves out of the box. Each time the children see a new scarf, have them call out what color it is. After the first child has 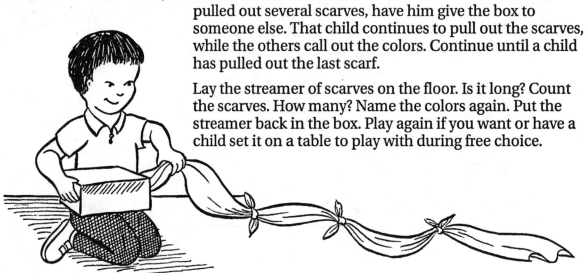 pulled out several scarves, have him give the box to someone else. That child continues to pull out the scarves, while the others call out the colors. Continue until a child has pulled out the last scarf.

Lay the streamer of scarves on the floor. Is it long? Count the scarves. How many? Name the colors again. Put the streamer back in the box. Play again if you want or have a child set it on a table to play with during free choice.

TALLER OR SHORTER

Activity

Have several children help you build a box tower in the middle of the circle time area. It should be about as tall as the height of your average child.

Sit with the children so everyone can see the tower. Have a child stand next to it. Ask the children to look at the child and the tower.

- If the child is taller than the tower, have the group call out *"taller."*

- If the child is shorter than the tower, call out *"shorter."*

- If the same, call out *"same."*

FAVORITE CEREAL CLUES

Activity

Have each child bring in an empty cereal box from his favorite cereal. *(Remember to write a quick note home or include the request in your family newsletter.)*

Set the cereal boxes in a row so the children can easily see them. *(If there are duplicates, group them together.)* Give a clue about one type of cereal, and see if the children guess what it is. If not, give them another clue. Continue giving clues until the children have guessed the cereal. Play again with a different cereal.

Extension

Cereal Box Construction – Put all the cereal boxes, glue, and brushes in the art area. Let the children glue the boxes together.

GUESS WHAT BOX

Activity

Gather several small objects that the children will probably recognize when they touch and feel them. Have a cube shaped tissue box. *(The opening is a perfect size for a child's hand.)*

Sit with the children. Secretly put one object in the box. Walk to each child. Have her close her eyes, reach into the box, and feel the object. After everyone has touched the object, talk about what it felt like *(small, hard, soft, squishy, textured, etc.)*, what it could be and why. Pull out the object and see what it is for real. Play again with a different object.

Variation

Secret Object – Each day let a different child pick a "secret" object and put it in the GUESS WHAT BOX. Play the game as above.

COLOR BOX

Activity

Get a medium size box. Glue a different colored piece of construction paper to each side.

Bring the box and a marker to circle time. Turn the box to all the sides and have the children call out each color. Pick one side, for example the red one, and say, *"Think of everything you know that is red."* As the children name things, write them on the red paper. Continue now or at another group with a different side. *(Remember to add things to your list that are 'red' as the children think of them.)* Continue the game until all the sides are written on. *(Set the box in the language area for the children to think about and "read.")*

OPEN THE DOOR

Activity

Get a medium size box. Cut a different size door on each side. *(Smallest one should be big enough to reach into the box.)* Put different size objects in the box.

Have a child come up to the box. Everyone say the OPEN THE DOOR chant.

OPEN THE DOOR

*Open the door, open the locks.
Let's take something out of the box.*

After the chant, have the child open the smallest door, feel the objects, and pull out something that fits through the door. Everyone call out what it is. Set the object on the floor. Say the chant and play again. Continue until all the objects are out of the box.

Variation

More OPEN THE DOOR Play – Instead of using random objects, use one category such as fruits. After the game, wash the fruits and have them for snack. Use miniature vehicles and afterwards take a walk around your neighborhood and look for real vehicles. And so on.

PREDICT AND CHECK

Activity

Before circle time, put the PREDICT AND CHECK box on a centrally located table. Tell the children, that as they are playing, they should look for things in the room that are magnetic and non-magnetic. Put them in the PREDICT AND CHECK box.

Bring the BOX and a magnet to circle time. Pull the objects out one at a time. Hold each one up and have the children predict if it will magnetize or not. Check their predictions by holding each object to the magnet. Have them call out *"yes"* if the object magnetized and *"no"* if it did not. After checking each one, have a child put the object back in the room where it belongs.

More Experimenting – Put the PREDICT AND CHECK box, several magnets and objects on a table for the children to experiment with on their own.

FEEL AND MATCH

Make the FEEL AND MATCH GAME

1. Cut a large, medium, and small triangle, circle, square, and rectangle out of fine sandpaper. Glue the shapes to a piece of poster board.

2. Cut a set of matching shapes out of coarse sandpaper. *(Optional: Back the shapes with posterboard.)* Put the shapes in a shallow box so they are easy to see.

Activity

Bring the board and shapes to circle time. Lay the board on the floor in the middle of the group. Have a child come up, pull a shape out of the box and hold it up for everyone to see. Call out its name. The child matches it to the identical shape on the game board. Continue playing until all the shapes are matched. *(Optional: After circle time put the game on the table for children to play by themselves or in small groups.)*

PEEK-A-BOO

Make a PEEK-A-BOO BOX

1. Get a medium or large size pizza box.

2. Divide the top of the box into 6-8 equal strips. Cut the strips, leaving each one attached to the side of the box.

3. Gather several large pictures or posters which fit in the box. Hide them in a bag.

Activity

Bring the pictures/posters and PEEK-A-BOO box to circle time. Have the children cover their eyes. Quickly slip a picture into the BOX (*such as a firefighter*). Tell the children

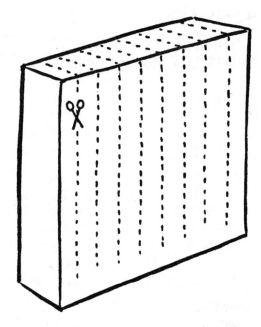

that there is a picture of a special person hiding in the PEEK-A-BOO box. You are going to slowly lift each strip, revealing a little bit of the person.

Open the first strip. *What do the children see? Does anyone want to guess who the person is?* Continue, slowly revealing more parts of the person until the children can name him/her. After the children know who it is, talk about all the things that fire fighters do.

Have the children cover their eyes. Slip another picture into the PEEK-A-BOO box and play again.

COLORED SNOWBALL COVER-UP

Activity

Get 5-8 different colored large pompoms and a small box.

Sit with the children. Line up the colored snowballs in front of you. Point to each one and have the children name its color. Have the children take one more look at the snowballs, and then cover their eyes. Hide one of the snowballs with the box. Have the children uncover their eyes, look at the snowballs, and call out the color of the snowball which is hiding. Lift the box off the snowball. Everyone call out the real color. Play again and again.

More Snowball Cover-up – To make the game more challenging, hide 2-3 snowballs under the one box or get several boxes and hide one snowball under each box.

WHAT'S IN THE BOX?

Activity

Collect two of a variety of objects *(ball, rubber band, brick, safety pin, bell)*. Put one of each object on a tray for the children to see. Put the second set in a bag. Have a box with a lid.

Turn your back on the children. Put one object from the bag into the box. Wrap a rubber band around the box to remind the children to keep the box closed. Turn around. Shake the box. Pass it to several children. *Do they think the object is heavy? What else do they think about the object? Looking at the objects on the tray, which one do they think is in the box?* Have the last child bring the box back to you. Ask if anyone else has anything to say before you open the box.

Open the box. Did they guess the match? Have a child take the object from the box and lay it next to the matching one on the tray. Repeat with the other objects.

PIZZA BOX STORIES

Make the PIZZA BOX FELT BOARD

Get clean pizza boxes from your local pizza restaurant. For each felt board cut a piece of felt the size of the lid. Glue it to the top.

Store the felt pieces for the story, rhyme, or activity in the box. Use a wide-diameter dowel rod to prop the lid open and keep it at a slight angle while using the board.

Activity

Enlarge and duplicate the 5 monkey patterns and back them with felt. Put them in the pizza box. Bring the pizza box to circle time. Prop the felt board up with the dowel rod.

Put the five monkeys on the board. Sing FIVE LITTLE MONKEYS JUMPING ON THE BED with the children. Each time one monkey falls off the bed, take a monkey off the felt board and put it in the box. *(Optional: Put the pizza box and felt pieces in the language area for the children to play with during free choice.)*

OLD MCDONALD HAD A FARM

Enlarge and duplicate the farm animals. Back them with felt. Put the animals in the pizza box. Pretend your felt board is Old McDonald's barnyard. Prop the board up with the dowel rod.

Start singing OLD McDONALD HAD A FARM. When you sing, *"… and on this farm he had a _____"* put one animal on the board and keep singing. Continue until Old McDonald has gathered all his animals in the barnyard.

ACTIVE GAMES

TAKE A FALL WALK

Make Simple COLLECTION BOXES

Get a large laundry detergent box with a handle for each child. Carefully cut off three sides of the top of each box, leaving the last side attached. Use a permanent marker to write each child's name on a box.

Activity

On a nice fall day, give each child his collection box and take a walk to a nearby park. On the way have the children look for signs of fall and put them in their boxes. When they get to the park, set the collection boxes around a tree. As the children play, have them continue to look for signs of fall and put them in their special boxes.

On the way back to school, have the children look for colored leaves. When each child finds a leaf he really likes, have him pick it up and carefully lay it in his box.

Let the children take their collection boxes home and show their families all the signs of fall they collected on their FALL WALK.

Variation

Fall Mural – Tape a piece of butcher paper to the art table. Have the children glue the fall objects from their boxes onto the paper and their special leaves around the outside edges for a border. Title it, and hang for all to look at and enjoy.

GRAB THE BOXES

Activity

Have your parachute/bed sheet and lots of small boxes in a bushel basket.

Lay the parachute on the floor and have the children stand around it. Have everyone hold the chute and slowly count *"1, 2, 3, 4, 5"* as they slowly lift it up. When the chute is at its highest, you go under the chute with the basket of boxes. Spread the boxes on the floor and leave the empty basket in the middle. Come back out and grab the side of the parachute. Help the children lower the chute to about waist-high as they count backwards, *"5, 4, 3, 2, 1."*

Now you're ready to play. The children count again and slowly raise the chute. This time, when the chute is over everyone's head, call on a child. That child quickly lets go of the chute, runs to the middle, grabs a box, puts it back in the basket, and goes back to his place on the chute. As the one child is going for the box, the rest of the children begin to slowly lower the chute while counting backwards, *"5, 4, 3, 2, 1."* The child grabbing the box tries to get back to his place before the chute is back at the children's waists. Continue playing until all of the boxes are back in the basket.

Extension

Drop the Box in the Basket – Put the boxes and basket in an untraveled area of the room. Let the children take all the boxes out of the basket and then drop them all back in.

Another Time – Put rubber bands around the boxes to keep their tops on. Toss the boxes in the basket.

BALANCING ACT

Activity

Pass out a different size box to each child. Ask one child to stand where everyone can easily see him. Have him balance his box on a part of his body, such as on his shoulder, knee, hand, or arm. Then encourage everyone to balance his box in the same place. *Why can or can't each person do this?* Maybe some boxes are too big to balance in that place.

Have another child balance her box, maybe on her head. Everyone copies her. Continue balancing until everyone who wants has led the BALANCING ACT.

MOVE TO THE NEXT ACTIVITY

Activity

Write 10-15 of your children's favorite transition time activities on strips of paper. Fold up each strip, and put it in a tiny box like a miniature slide-type match box. Put

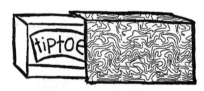

the tiny boxes in a basket and set it near your circle time area.

At the end of each circle time have a child get the basket and pick one of the boxes. Slowly open it up and pull out the strip. Read the activity. Do it as the transition activity from group to the next activity on the daily schedule.

POSSIBLE TRANSITION ACTIVITIES

- Choose your favorite animal and move like it to _____. *(Each child does.)*

- Tiptoe to _____. Shh, the dolls are sleeping. *(Name each child and remind him to tiptoe.)*

- Play FROGGIE IN THE MIDDLE. *(After each pair of children has hopped in the middle, have them hop out of the group to the next activity each is going to do.)*

- Drive your favorite vehicle to _____. *(Have each child name a vehicle [tractor, truck, police car, taxi, motorcycle, etc.] and then drive it to the next activity.)*

- Speed walk to _____. *(Name each child or pair of children and have him/them speed walk.)*

- Tightrope walk to _____. *(Each child does.)*

- Pretend you're walking in quicksand to _____. *(Each child does.)*

- Play SIMON SAYS. *(Tell each child where and how to move.)*

- March/skip to the next activity singing "High-ho, high-ho, it's off to work we go…" *(Each child does.)*

- Swim like a fish to _____. *(Each child does.)*

- Play STOP AND GO. *(Have a red and green circle. Walk to each child and hold up the red or green circle. If it is green that child can go to the next activity. If red she must stay at group. By the end to the game, you have shown a green circle to each child.)*

- Hum a lullaby, such as ROCK-A-BYE-BABY, as you tiptoe to _____. *(Ask each child what he is going to hum, and where he is moving to.)*

- Play CHUG-A-CHUG. *(Form a train with all the children. "Chug" around the room, dropping off the passengers at the places they want.)*

- Ride a horse to _____. *(Each child does.)*

- Think of your favorite animal and wag your tail as you go to _____. *(Each child names a favorite animal and wags its tail as he moves.)*

- IT'S RAINING! *(Have each child hold an umbrella over her head as she moves to the next activity.)*

- Buzz like bees to _____. *(Each child does.)*

PASS THE BOX

Activity

Before circle time, put something in a box which makes a fairly distinctive noise or maybe no noise, when you shake it *(bell, dried corn, spoon, nail, rice, cotton ball)*. Cover the box and wrap a rubber band around it.

Begin the music. *(If you're playing this during a holiday season, use holiday music.)* Start passing the box around the circle. Stop the music. The child who's holding the box shakes it for everyone to hear. *What could it be?* Start the music again and continue passing the box. Stop the music. That child shakes it for everyone to hear. *What do you think? Any other ideas?* Do several more times. Everyone guesses what might be in the box. Open the box for everyone to see what it really is.

BOX FIELD TRIP

Activity

Make arrangements with a local department store, which offers a gift wrapping service, to have one of the gift wrappers visit your classroom. Ask him or her to bring samples of the different size boxes and types of wrapping papers s/he uses for gifts. Encourage the children to think of gifts that would fit in each of the boxes and what wrapping paper they would like to use for their gifts.

Variation

"Box" Field Trip – Take the children to a department store which offers gift wrapping. Divide into small groups, and watch the gift wrappers wrap the boxes in all types of fancy paper, ribbon, and bows.

MITTEN TOSS

Make the MITTEN TOSS GAME

1. **Gameboard** – Get a small, medium, and large size box top. Use colored markers to draw and color a small, medium, and a large snow pal in the appropriate box top.

2. **Mitten Beanbags** – Get 8-10 old mittens. Fill them with dried beans. Tie them tightly closed. Put the mittens in a bucket.

Activity

Bring the snow pal box tops and mitten beanbags to circle time. Put the boxes in the middle of the group area. Pass out the mittens. Have each child tell which snow pal he is going to toss his mitten into and then toss it. Play several times, encouraging the children to "aim" for different boxes. *(After circle time, put the game in an untraveled area of the classroom. Let the children play MITTEN TOSS during free choice.)*

EXERCISE IN A BOX

Activity

Duplicate the BEND AND STRETCH CHART. Hang it at the children's eye level on a wall which has open space around it. Get a large box top or cut down a large box so that it has about a 3" lip. Put the box/box top on the floor in front of the BEND AND STRETCH CHART. Securely tape it to the floor.

Encourage the children to EXERCISE IN THE BOX. They can copy the kittens, make up their own exercises, exercise in pairs, etc. Here are several exercises to help children begin.

- Jump inside the box.
- March in the box.
- Run in place in the box.
- Jump up and down with a partner in the box.
- Crawl around the box.
- Tiptoe around the edge of the box.
- Hop on one foot in the box.

BEND AND STRETCH

OBSTACLE COURSE

Activity

Collect all types of boxes and use them to make an obstacle course around your room. Introduce the children to the COURSE during a circle time and then leave it set up for children to use during free choice. See the two illustrations for possible paths and set ups.

Small Area Obstacle Course

(classroom)

Large Area Obstacle Course

(outside, gym, empty room)

GO FOR THE GREEN

Activity

Get a divided box from the grocery store. Cut it down so it is about 5"-6" high. Paint it with green tempera paint. Collect a variety of green collage materials *(bows, yarn, string, fabric, wallpaper pieces, etc.)* for an art activity. Save one of each material. Hide the rest around the room before the children come to school.

At the first circle time of the day, have the green box and the sample of each green material. Show the children each green material and then put it in one section of your box. After you've shown them all the materials, have a child put the green box on the art table.

At the end of circle time, play GO FOR THE GREEN. Tell the children that when you say, *"Go for the green"* they should get up and begin searching throughout the room for more green materials. As they find the materials, have the children put them in the appropriate sections of the green box.

After all of the materials have been found, tape a large piece of butcher paper to the table and let the children make a GO FOR THE GREEN collage.

WHERE'S THE BOX

Activity

Sit in a circle on the floor. Have a small box. Give it to a child and ask her to balance it somewhere on herself. Have the others call out where she is balancing it. She hands the box to another person. That person balances it somewhere else. Continue for as long as you want. *(As the children gain skill, go faster and faster.)*

LOOK AROUND YOUR NEIGHBORHOOD

Make BINOCULARS With the Children

Help each child make a pair of binoculars.
To make each pair:

1. Have each child paint two toilet paper rolls and let them dry.

2. After the toilet paper rolls have dried, help each child glue her pair together. Let dry.

3. Punch a hole on each side of the glued toilet paper rolls.

4. Loop a long piece of yarn through the holes, so the "binoculars" will easily hang around the child's neck.

Activity

On a nice day take a walk around your neighborhood. Have the children wear their binoculars.

Stop along the way and use them.

- Look up in the tree. *What do you see? Birds? Leaves? Branches?*

- Look at the clouds. *How are they moving? See any shapes – Dog? Elephant?*

- See an ant hill? Stop and look at it through the binoculars. *Do you see any ants?*

- Look at the ducks on the water. *What are they doing? Flying? Talking to each other? Swimming?*

BOX CONSTRUCTIONS

Activity

Put a large piece of cardboard on the floor in the middle of the circle time area. Collect enough boxes so that each child has at least one. Bring them all to circle time.

Pass out the boxes. Tell the children that they are going to help each other build a tower, house, or an imaginary structure with their boxes. You start by putting the first box on the piece of cardboard. *(Do it.)* Let each child add a box until all the boxes are on the piece of cardboard. Talk about the structure.

Now ask a child to remove one box from the structure, trying not to let any of the other boxes move. Continue, letting the children carefully take off one box at a time. After all the boxes have been removed, call on a child to begin the building process again. When finished, talk about the new structure and compare it to what the children remember about the first one. *(After circle time put the boxes in the block area and encourage the children to continue building.)*

BUSTER BOXES

Make the BUSTER BOXES

1. Get six same size small boxes such as six shoe boxes or large tissue boxes *(cut off tops)*.

2. Duplicate Buster's face six times. Color him.

3. Staple/glue him to the front end of each box.

Activity

Have a bucket of ping pong or yarn balls. Place the 6 BUSTER BOXES in a row. Have a child stand behind the first box. Give him a ping pong ball or yarn ball. Let him toss the ball into any box. When he does, everyone claps. Give a ball to a second child. Let her toss the ball into a box. Clap again. Continue. At the end, count all of the balls in each BUSTER BOX.

Pass out the balls and play again. Encourage the children to toss their ball/s into different BUSTER BOXES. *(After circle time, put the BUSTER BOXES in a quiet area of the room for the children to use during free choice.)*

SIMON SAYS

Activity

Bring a box filled with different size cardboard tubes *(toilet paper, wrapping paper, paper towels, fax paper, etc.)* to circle time. Let the children each choose one or two tubes and pretend they are barbells used in exercising. Play SIMON SAYS. Simon will give the exercising directions.

- Simon says, *"Move the barbells up and down five times over your head. Let's count as we lift the barbells."*

- Simon says, *"Slowly wave the barbells at your side."*

- Simon says, *"Do frontwards arm rolls with your barbells. Backwards."*

- Simon says, *"Oh the barbells are so heavy! Lift them slowly over your head … Rest."*

- Simon says, *"March the barbells in front of you."*

- Continue in this way. Maybe the children would like to switch barbells and/or take turns being Simon.

DUMP THE MARBLES

Activity

Give each child a small box. Have one marble in your box. Start the music. Pass the marble to the person next to you by "dumping" it in his box. That person turns to the person next to him and dumps the marble again.

Continue dumping the marble in the person's box next to you, until the music stops. Give the child, holding the marble in his box, another marble. He puts the marble in his box, the music starts again, and he dumps two marbles in the child's box next to him. Continue playing in this manner, adding another marble each time you stop the music.

WALK THE PLANK

Activity

Fill lots of small boxes with beans. Glue the tops securely to the bottoms. Put the boxes in a shoe box. Place the balance beam in the middle of the circle time area.

Pass the shoe box around, and let each child pick a box. Have one child stand at each end of the balance beam. They should balance their boxes on their bodies, and then begin to WALK THE PLANK. When they reach the middle they can get off or try to walk backwards to the beginning of the PLANK. Clap for each pair of children.

STACK THE BOXES

Activity

Choose five to seven different size boxes. Lay them in a line going from largest to smallest. Talk about the sizes. Begin to stack the boxes with the children, putting the largest one on the bottom. Have a child take the next one and put it on top of the largest one. Continue until all the boxes are stacked. Count the boxes. *Will they fall?*

Let the children take the boxes down one at a time. Stack it again. Let the children pick the order. Watch what happens. *Is it going to fall? Why? Why not?*

COLORFUL MOBILE

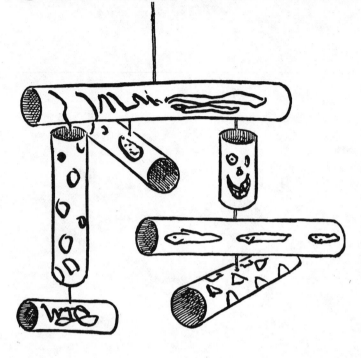

You'll Need

- All sizes of cardboard tubes (*toilet paper, wrapping paper, paper towel, aluminum foil, etc.*)
- Tempera paint/brushes

Activity

Put all the cardboard tubes in a large box so the children can easily see them. Set the box near the easel. Let the children clip the tubes to the easel and paint them. Have a special place for the children to stand their painted tubes to dry.

Extension

Display the Tubes In the Room

- Make them into a mobile and hang from the ceiling.
- Make them into a long "rope" and border your bulletin board or door.

BOX MOLDS

Make BOX MOLDS

Collect all sizes of sturdy dairy boxes – cottage cheese, milk, cream, yogurt, etc. Cut off all attached tops from the boxes. Wash and dry the boxes and all usable lids. Put them in a shallow box.

Activity

Set the box of molds, rolling pins, and batch of soft dough on the table. Let the children roll out the dough and use the boxes to "cut" as many shapes as they'd like.

FINGER PAINTING AT THE EASEL

You'll Need

🔷 Tempera paint/finger paint

🔷 Evaporated milk *(optional)*

🔷 Several quart milk boxes

🔷 Finger paint paper

🔷 1 small spray bottle of water for each easel

Activity

Cut off one side of each milk box. Pour finger paint into each box. Stir in a little evaporated milk. *(Makes paint glossy.)* Set the paint boxes and spray bottles in the easel trays.

Have each child clip a piece of paper to the easel and then spray his paper with water. Encourage him to finger paint for as long as he wants, using as many different colors as he would like.

Hints

🔷 Have him count *"1, 2, 3"* as he pumps the spray bottle to wet-down his paper.

🔷 If the paper gets too dry, have him spray it with *"1"* pump and then continue to paint.

BOX COLLAGE

You'll Need

🔷 Medium, sturdy box

🔷 Collage/art box

🔷 Glue/paste

🔷 Brushes

Activity

Set all the supplies on the art table. Let the children glue/paste the various materials on the box. *(You might want to let this activity continue for several days.)* After the box is dry, hang it from your ceiling for everyone to enjoy and talk about.

MARBLE PAINTING

You'll Need

- Marbles
- Margarine tubs
- Cylindrical boxes such as oatmeal, chips, corn meal, etc.
- Spoons
- Tempera paint
- White duplicating paper

Activity

Pour different colors of paint into the margarine tubs. Add several marbles and a spoon to each tub. Set the supplies on the art table.

When a child comes to the activity, have him roll up a piece of paper and put it in a cylinder box. Let him roll the marbles around in the paint and spoon them into the box. Then put the top on the container, and begin to shake, roll, and tip the box back and forth. After a while, dump the marbles back into the paint, roll them around again, put them back in the box, and shake some more. When the child is finished, have him take his painting out of the cylinder, let it dry, and then hang it up.

SPICE BOX PRINTING

You'll Need

- Different sizes of metal spice boxes
- Metal bandage boxes
- Tempera paint
- Paper

Activity

Pour shallow amounts of different colors of paint into foam vegetable trays. Put them on the art table. Let the children dip the tops/bottoms of the boxes into the paint and make prints all over their papers.

Another Time – Use dairy boxes *(small milk cartons, yogurt, cottage cheese, etc.)* instead of spice boxes.

TEXTURED BOX PRINTING

You'll Need

- Juice concentrate cans
- Round dairy boxes *(soft cheese, yogurt)*
- Heavy yarn/twine/bric-brac
- Large pieces of paper *(newspaper works well)*
- Tempera paint

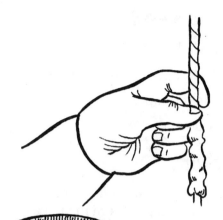

Make TEXTURED BOXES

1. Dip the yarn/twine/bric-brac in glue. Wipe off the excess glue from each piece.
2. Wrap sticky yarn/twine/bric-brac around the boxes. Let dry overnight.

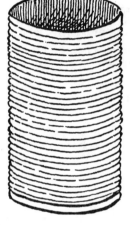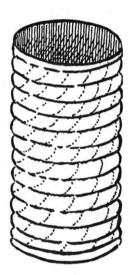

Activity

Pour shallow amounts of paint on large styrofoam vegetable trays. Put these and the TEXTURED BOXES on the art table.

Let the children roll the TEXTURED BOXES in paint and then print designs on their paper. Encourage the children to use different colors and try the different prints.

After the activity, wash the textured boxes so they are ready to use another day.

Another Time – Glue different textures to the boxes and print with these *(styrofoam peanuts, corrugated cardboard, coffee stirrers, etc.)*.

ICE CHUNK PAINTING

You'll Need

- Small dairy boxes
- Dry tempera paint in unbreakable salt shakers
- Butcher paper
- Mittens

Activity

Make giant ice cubes in different dairy boxes. Just before the activity, take them out of the boxes and put them in an ice chest. Tape a long sheet of butcher paper to the table. Put the ice chest, dry paint, and mittens near the table.

Let the children shake all colors of dry tempera on the paper. Then put on their mittens, pick up one or two ice chunks, and slowly move them through the paint. Watch the paint colors come alive as they mix with each other. When each child finishes, have her put the ice chunk/s back in the ice chest so it is ready for another child.

Variation

Paint With Giant Popsicles – To make the popsicles, stick a tongue depressor in the giant cubes after they have partially frozen. Let them completely freeze, pop them out of the molds, and put them in the ice chest as you did above.

POUR AND PAINT

You'll Need

- Small brushes *(Paste brushes work well because they have short handles and stubby brushes.)*
- Styrofoam egg cartons
- Small pitchers/measuring cups with spouts
- Tempera paint
- Paper

Activity

Cut the egg cartons into 4 and 6 cup sections. Pour different colors of tempera paint into the pitchers. Set the egg cartons, pitchers of paint, paper, and brushes on the art table. *(You could also have a small bucket of water to keep the brushes clean during the activity.)*

When a child wants to paint, let him pour the colors he wants into his own egg carton container, get several brushes, and choose his paper. Let him paint for as long as he'd like.

RAINWATER PAINTING

You'll Need

- Several juice boxes
- Watercolor sets/ brushes

Activity

Cut one large side off all the juice boxes. On a rainy day, have the children help you set them on a tray. Carry the tray outside and set it in an open area, so the rain easily collects in the boxes.

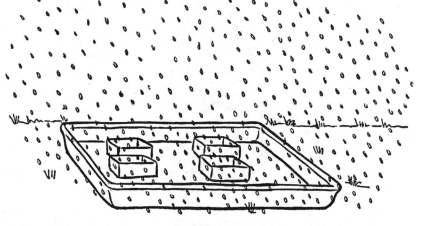

After the rain, go outside and get the boxes. Set them on the art table along with the watercolor paints and paper. Let the children paint for as long as they want using their special rainwater.

SUN CRAYONS

You'll Need

🔷 Styrofoam egg cartons   🔷 Old crayons   🔷 Tray   🔷 Butcher paper

Activity

Gather all the old crayons. Have the children help you peel off the paper on each one. Break the crayons into small pieces. Put several crayon stubs in each egg cup. *(Use as many egg cartons as you need.)* When you go outside, have the children carry the egg cartons and the tray. Set the egg cartons on the tray. Put the tray in an untraveled place in the sun. Watch what happens to the crayons. Gently cover them and let them harden overnight.

First thing the next morning, walk outside with the children and see the crayons. Bring the egg cartons inside. Let the children help you pop out the new crayons. Put them in a special basket. Tape a large sheet of butcher paper to the art table. Let the children draw and scribble with their new SUN CRAYONS.

HARVEST COLLAGE

You'll Need

🔷 Small box tops *(gift boxes, shoe boxes)*   🔷 Glue/paste

Activity

Get a large bag or basket and take an autumn walk with the children. As you walk, have the children pick up colored leaves, twigs, acorns, pebbles, etc. and put them in the bag.

When you get back to the classroom, put all the items on the table. As each child chooses, let her make a fall collage by gluing some of her favorite items to a box top. When she's finished, ask her if she wants to say anything about the fall items or the walk. If she does, write what she says in the box top or on a piece of paper which you can staple to the box top.

SCRAP BOX MURAL

You'll Need

- 4-6 shoe boxes
- Butcher paper

Fill the SCRAP BOXES

Tape shoe boxes around the edges of your art table. As the children are doing art activities, have them put their "good scraps" in the boxes. Do this for several weeks or until the boxes are full. *(Have one box on the art shelf for even bigger scraps.)*

Activity

When one or two SCRAP BOXES are full of scraps, tape a large sheet of butcher paper to the art table. Have glue/paste and the SCRAP BOX/ES on the table. Let the children stick all the "scraps" to the paper. When finished, hang the SCRAP BOX MURAL for everyone to see.

Variation

One day put your large collage box on the table. Untape one shoe box. Have the children help you sort the different scraps and put them in the sections of the collage box. After the scraps in the first shoe box have been sorted, untape another shoe box and sort those scraps. Continue until all sections of the collage box are full of a variety of scraps. Use to make another mural.

EASY PAINT TOTES

You'll Need

- Divided soda boxes
- 6-8 juice concentrate boxes with lids

Activity

Put a juice concentrate box in each section of the soda box. Pour a different color paint in each container. Cover them so the paint stays fresh.

Use the PAINT TOTE to easily carry paint to wherever the activity is – at the art table, on the floor, outside, etc. After the children have used all the paint in a concentrate box, simply throw it away and fill a clean one. *(The TOTES are so handy, you'll probably need several.)*

COLORED SAND DESIGNS

You'll Need

- 4-5 half gallon milk boxes
- Sand
- Different colors of chalk
- Unbreakable salt shakers
- Heavy duty paper such as cardboard
- Glue in small bottles

Activity

(this could be a two day activity)

Color the Sand

Cut down the milk boxes so they form 2" high boxes. Put a little sand and several pieces of the same color chalk in each box.

Set the milk boxes on the art table. Let the children color the sand by rubbing the chalk back and forth over the sand. Every once in a while shake the sand to mix the color. Keep chalking until the sand is completely colored. Using a funnel, pour each color of sand into a different salt shaker.

Colored Sand Designs

Put the paper, salt shakers, an empty pie pan, and glue bottles on the table. Let the children drizzle glue on their paper and then shake colored sand over it. After the children have shaken the colored sand along their trails, have them shake the excess sand into the empty pie pan. *(In the end you could pour the multi-colored sand in a salt shaker and shake it along the drizzle trails.)* Let the glue designs dry.

BOX FRAMES

You'll Need

- Gift boxes
- Shoe boxes
- Tissue boxes
- Different size sturdy boxes
- Watered-down white glue

Activity

Frame children's art with boxes.

- **Large Box Frame** – Cut openings in gift boxes to fit the size of the art. Brush glue around the edge of the art and glue it to the inside of the box.

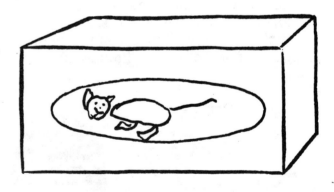

- **Small Box Frame** – Frame small pieces of art in tissue boxes which already have the top cut out.

- **Art Stack** – Stack sturdy boxes. Glue them together. Display art on all sides of each box. Great for the entrance to the room or tucked next to the book shelf.

Art Mobile – Get two large branches. Criss-cross them and tie them in the middle. Hang the branches from your ceiling. Tie different length heavy twine to the branches. Have different boxes. Glue artwork on all sides of a box. Clip each box to a piece of twine.

LEARNING CENTERS

QUICK SCOOPS, BUCKETS AND MOLDS

Make QUICK SCOOPS

1. Get pint, quart, and half gallon milk boxes. Tape the tops securely closed.

2. Lay the boxes on their sides. Starting at the top of each box, cut diagonally to the bottom to form a scoop shape.

Make QUICK BUCKETS

1. Get half gallon and gallon milk boxes.

2. Cut the tops off the boxes so they are different depths ranging from several inches to 5 or 6 inches.

3. Add rope handles to each bucket.

Make QUICK SAND MOLDS

1. Get different sizes and shapes of small dairy boxes such as milk, cottage cheese, and juice concentrate.

2. Cut them down if necessary.

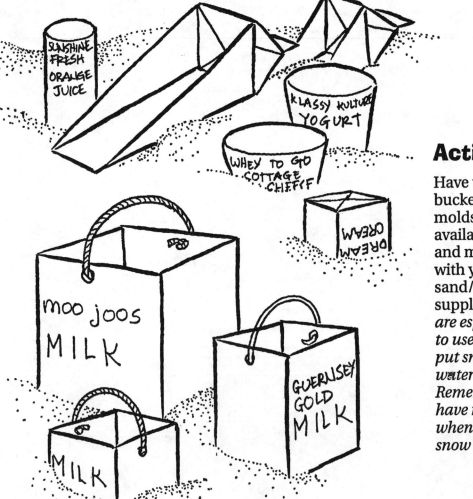

Activity

Have the scoops, buckets, and molds always available. Mix and match them with your other sand/water supplies. (These are especially fun to use when you put snow in your water table. Remember to have mittens when you set up snow play.)

TEDDY BEAR FEEL AND FIND

Activity

Get 2 shoe box tops. Put 15-21 colored dots on the underside of each top. Have your sand table filled about half to three-fourths full of sand. Hide as many teddy bears as you have dots on your shoe box tops. Put one top at each end of the sand table.

Let the children feel around the sand looking for teddy bears. When a child finds one, she should take it out and set it on one of the colored dots. Children can easily come and go from the activity, playing until all of the colored dots have teddy bears on them. Set up the game again, letting the children help you hide the teddy bears and then FEEL AND FIND them.

BOAT FLOAT

Make SIMPLE BOATS

1. Cut down small milk and cream boxes.

2. Tape or glue flags to the side of each boat.

Activity

Float the boats in the water table or a small children's plastic pool. Add people and supplies *(colored inch blocks, soda caps, tiny twigs, etc.)*.

Variation

More BOAT FLOAT – Other times include different types of boats such as: sections from egg cartons, styrofoam plates, cut-down styrofoam cups, salad bar boxes, etc.

HANGING FUNNELS AND SIEVES

Make FUNNELS

1. Get a quart or half gallon milk box. Tape the top securely closed.
2. Cut a 1/2" notch in the top of the box.
3. Cut off the bottom of the box.
4. Punch a hole on two opposite sides of the milk box about an inch from the bottom. Slip a long rope through the holes.

Make SIEVES

1. Get a quart or half gallon milk box. Tape the top securely closed.
2. Carefully punch small holes on all sides of the top half of the box.
3. Cut off the bottom of the box.
4. Punch a hole on two opposite sides of the milk box about an inch from the bottom. Slip a long rope through the holes.

Activity

Hang the sieves and/or funnels from the ceiling over the water table. *(Have sand or water in the table.)* Have small pitchers, scoops, spoons, and measuring cups in the table. Let the children pour and scoop the sand/water into the funnels and sieves. Watch what happens.

SINK AND FLOAT

Activity

Fill the sand/water table with water. Get 6-8 quart and half gallon milk boxes. Cut them down so they have different heights.

Put the boxes in the water table with several small pitchers and scoops. Let the children blow the boxes around the water. Encourage them to add a little water to the boxes. *Can they still sail them? Add a little more water. What happens? How much water do they need to add before the boxes begin to sink?* Let the children continue to experiment on their own. Add and subtract supplies as the children need them.

Extension

Play Some More – Another time have several small buckets of pebbles, bottle caps, or marbles. Let the children sink and float the boats with them.

OCEAN LIFE

You'll Need

- Variety of homemade/rubber ocean creatures
- Seaweed
- Rocks
- Sand
- Shells

Activity

Fill your sand/water table about half to three-fourths full of water. Add a little sand to lay on the bottom. Set the seaweed in the sand. Lay the rocks and shells around.

Let the children explore the ocean environment, feel the seaweed, help the fish swim, search for seashells, etc.

Extension

Look More Carefully – Make several periscopes. Put them on a shelf next to the water table. Show the children how to gently slide them into the water, wait for the water to calm down, and then look through the periscopes. Talk with the children about what they see – sand, rocks, shells, seaweed, etc.

To Make Each Periscope

1. Cut off the top and bottom of a milk box.

2. Lay a long piece of plastic wrap on the table. Set the milk box in the middle of the wrap.

3. Bring the wrap up the sides of the box and tuck them into the top. Tape the wrap inside the top of the box.

4. Slip several rubber bands up the carton to help hold the plastic wrap tightly to the sides.

OCEAN CREATURE PATTERNS

(Make ocean creatures using these patterns and heavy-weight colored vinyl material from old school notebooks.)

For additional water animal patterns see page 35 in the PLAY WITH BIG BOXES book.

TAKE YOUR FAVORITE DOLL FOR A RIDE

Activity

Get a shoe box. Poke a small hole in one end and stick a three foot piece of rope through it. Attach the rope to the box by tying a knot on the inside of the box. Tie a loop handle in the other end of the rope.

Let a child put a pillow and blanket in the box, and/or her favorite doll or stuffed animal. Pull the doll/animal around the room or outside play area. The child may also want to carry things for her doll to play with and/or a baby bottle in case her baby gets thirsty along the way.

Variation

Shoe Box Beds – Get several shoe boxes. Cut pieces of foam rubber to fit in the bottom of each one. Add pillows and blankets. *(Beanbags make good pillows.)*

READ BIRTHDAY CARDS

Activity

Cut down a laundry soap concentrate box so that it is about 4" high. Cover it with cheerful self-adhesive paper. Save birthday cards. Put them in the box.

Set the box of cards in the housekeeping area. Encourage the children to READ THE BIRTHDAY CARDS to each other and their babies.

Variation

Holiday Cards – Collect cards of different holidays your children celebrate. Put these cards in special boxes. For example, Valentine cards in a heart shaped box, Thanksgiving cards in a turkey gift box, etc.

FOOD IN THE HOUSE

Activity

Collect empty food boxes *(cereal, rice, gelatin, etc.)*. Put them in the housekeeping cupboard. Encourage the children to use them as they fix meals and snacks for their "children and guests."

SOCKS BOX

Activity

Fill a box with different pairs of socks. Set it in the housekeeping area. Let the children match the pairs and fold them.

TALK ON THE TELEPHONE

Activity

Get several quart size milk boxes. Cut a 1"x 4" opening in the center area of two opposite sides of each box. On a small piece of solid color self adhesive paper make the dial. Stick it to the middle of one solid side of the box. *(Repeat for each box.)*

Put the telephones in the housekeeping area. Encourage the children to call each other and chit-chat, practice emergency calls, invite each other to birthday parties, order pizzas, etc.

SNACK-IN-A-BOX

Activity

Have the ingredients for a very simple snack on a tray. Bring the tray into the housekeeping area and make snack with the children. Put the snack in individual boxes and have it ready to serve at snack time.

Popcorn – Make popcorn with the children. Put it in several popcorn boxes. At snack time, pass the boxes of popcorn and let each child scoop a little on his plate.

Energy Snack – Gather a variety of small boxes – one for each child. Mix pretzels, raisins, and cereals in a big bowl. Let the children scoop some energy snack into each box. Pass them at snack time.

Favorite Cereal – Have a clean yogurt box for each child. Pour a little cereal into each one. At snack let the children each take a cereal box and pour milk in it. Um! Good!

Box Pops – Get a small empty juice concentrate box for each child. Cut them down if you like. Fill each one about half full of cranberry, grapefruit, lime, or grape juices. Put the BOX POPS in the freezer. When the POPS begin to harden, put a popsicle stick into each one. Let the POPS completely freeze. At snack, let each child pull his JUICE POP out of the box and eat it. *(Great snack on a warm day.)*

PLAY IN THE DOLL HOUSE

Make a Simple DOLL HOUSE

1. Get a large, divided box such as one that a dozen 2-3 liter soda bottles come in. Cut off the cover of the box. Turn the box on its side.

2. Make large rooms in the house by cutting away several of the cardboard dividers. *(If the rooms are too deep, turn the box back over and cut more off the top.)*

3. Optional – Glue pieces of carpeting to the floors and wallpaper to the walls.

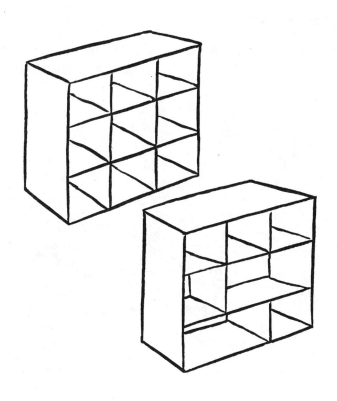

Activity

Set the doll house, furniture, people, and vehicles on the table. Let the children set up the rooms anyway they choose and then play HOUSE.

LUNCH BOX MAGNET FUN

Activity

Get several metal lunch boxes. Put magnetic pieces inside *(numbers, letters, figures, characters, animals, shapes)*. Put the boxes on the shelf.

Have the children set the LUNCH BOX/ES on the floor or table. Open the box. The cover is the magnet board. Let the children use the magnetic pieces however they choose –

- To tell stories
- To name pieces
- To play a game with a friend.

When finished, the children simply put the pieces back in the lunch box, close it up, and put it back on the shelf.

ME BOXES

Make ME BOXES With The Children

1. Have each child bring his favorite cereal box to school.
2. Cut large gingerbread figures out of whatever color construction paper each child chooses.
3. Let them "dress" their figures however they want. Help each child staple his figure to the front of his cereal box.
4. Cut lots of small construction paper gingerbread characters. Keep them in a small box with a marker or pencil.

Activity

Have the children tell you different things about themselves during free choice. Write each thing they tell you on a different small gingerbread character. Then let the children slip the figures into their boxes. *(This is an ongoing activity. Periodically ask the children if they would like to take the ME BOXES home to share with their families.)*

104

MAIL A LETTER

Make the LETTER BOXES

1. Collect 6 cylinder-type boxes (*oatmeal, corn meal, etc.*). Remove the lids. Cover the boxes with blue adhesive or construction paper.

2. On the first box print ABCD, on the second box print EFGH, on the third print IJKL, on the fourth MNOP, on the fifth QRSTU, and on the sixth VWXYZ.

3. Glue a piece of red construction paper to the top of each lid. Cut a large slit in each one. Put the lids back on the boxes.

4. Glue the 6 letter boxes to a piece of sturdy cardboard.

5. Make the letters. Cut at least 26, 2"x 3" posterboard cards. Print a letter on each one. Put them in a margarine tub waiting to be mailed.

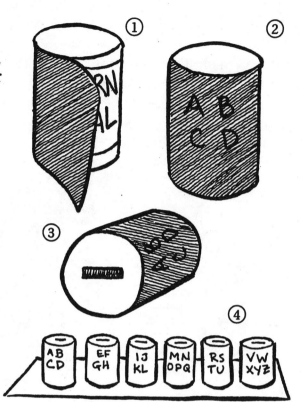

Activity

Set the game on the floor/table in the language area. When the "letter carriers" come to work, have them put on their letter carrier headbands, take out all the letters, and mail them in the letter boxes.

NAME BLOCKS

Activity

Get enough plastic photo cube boxes so that there are enough sides for each child to have one. *(Thus one cube is enough for 6 children.)* Cut construction paper squares to fit in each side. Write one child's name on each square. Slip it into the box.

Put all the NAME BLOCKS on the language shelf. Encourage the children to play with them however they choose.

They could roll them to each other and read the names.

They could stack them on the floor and find different names.

They could try to name the letters.

They could play I SPY A NAME. One child reads a name and another one tries to find it.

FAVORITE WORD BOXES

Make the FAVORITE WORD BOXES

1. Collect one crayon/chalk/raisin box with a flip top for each child. Cover the fronts of the boxes with plain colored adhesive paper. *(You could also use small dairy boxes. Simply cut three sides off the top so that it flips up. Cover the front side just like you did the crayon box.)*

2. Print each child's name on a box.

3. Slightly glue the FAVORITE WORD BOXES to a piece of posterboard. Hang the posterboard on a wall at the children's eye level.

4. Cut lots of 2"x 4" pieces of posterboard for the WORD CARDS.

Activity

Encourage the children to tell you their favorite words. Print each one on a card. As you print the word/s say each letter to the child. Have him slip his CARD/S into his BOX. When it is full, carefully remove it from the posterboard and let the child take it home. Glue another box on the posterboard so he can add more FAVORITE WORDS.

THROUGH THE TUNNELS

Activity

Get a variety of sizes of milk boxes. Cut the top, bottom, and one side off each box to make the tunnels. Tape a long masking tape road on your floor or edge of a long table. Put the tunnels along the road. Have a basket of small vehicles.

Let the children drive the different vehicles along the road. Be flexible as the children play. Maybe they will want to move the tunnels. Maybe they will want a second road. *(Each time you set up this activity, "build" the road with new corners, sharper and wider curves, longer and shorter straightaways, etc.)*

CLIP THE CLIPS

Activity

Fill a shoe box or shoe box top with a wide variety of different clips *(butterfly clips, office clips, spring- loaded clothespins, hair clips, chip clips, paper clips, etc.)*.

Put the CLIP THE CLIPS game on the table/floor. Let the children play individually or with a friend. Encourage the player/s to clip as many clips as he can around the edge of the box/box top. When he's done, unclip the clips and put them back in the box for the next player.

CLIP THE CLOTHESPINS

Activity

Fill a shoe box with different colored clothespins. Tie one end of a piece of heavy yarn around the middle of the shoe box. Securely tape the other end to the underside of a table.

Let the children sit under the table and CLIP THE CLOTHESPINS to the yarn. Then unclip them and put them back in the box.

After the children are familiar with the game:

- Encourage them to play in pairs.

- Make patterns with the clothespins.

- Play COPY CAT – I clip a clothespin. You match it.

- Play I'LL CLIP ONE–YOU CLIP ONE. Take turns clipping clothespins until you reach the top of the yarn, and then reverse it and take turns unclipping the clothespins until you get to the bottom.

COLOR DROP

Make Quick
COLOR DROP BOXES

1. Get poker chips of two or three different colors and a large cylinder box with a lid. Cover the box with a colorful adhesive paper. (*To make the game more difficult, use smaller chips such as bingo chips.*)

2. Cut two or three slits in the lid, large enough for the poker chips to easily slip through. (*Cut smaller slits to accommodate the smaller chips.*)

3. Color the slits to match the color of the chips.

4. Put all the poker chips in the box.

Activity

Put the COLOR DROP BOX on the table. Dump the chips out. Let a child slip the poker chips through the slits into the box. Encourage her to match them to the colors of the slits.

MISSING PIECES BOX

Make a
MISSING PIECES BOX

1. Get a sturdy shallow gift box.

2. Cut a large construction paper oval. Write MISSING PIECES BOX on the oval. Staple it to one of the edges.

Activity

Set the MISSING PIECES BOX in a central easy-to-reach place. When the children find pieces to games, puzzles, or objects they don't recognize, have them put the missing pieces in the special box. Sometime during each day talk with the children about each "thing" in the box. If a child recognizes it, have her return it to its place.

LACE AND TIE

Activity

Get a shoe box lid. Using the shoe pattern, draw a shoe picture on the inside of the lid. Punch the holes for the shoe lace. Tie a shoe lace through one of the bottom holes. *(Make several LACE AND TIE boards.)*

Put the LACE AND TIE boards on the housekeeping table. Let the children lace the shoes and then practice tying and untying them.

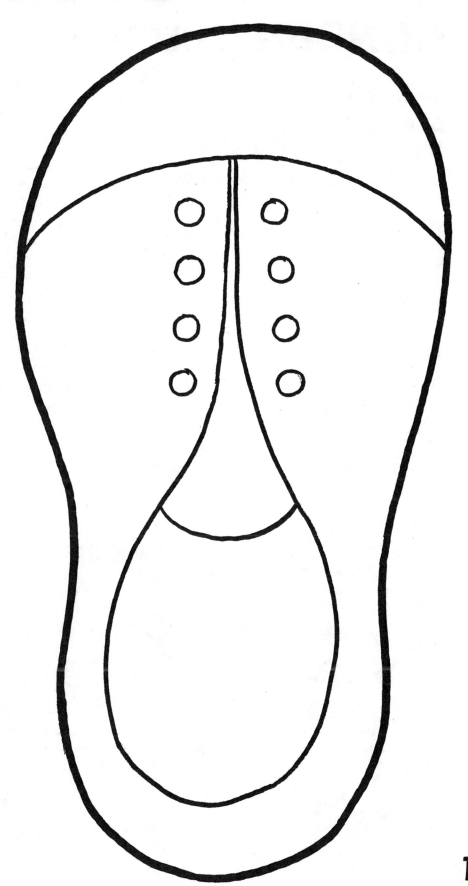

EXERCISE PUPPY CONCENTRATION

Make the EXERCISE PUPPY CONCENTRATION GAME

1. Get 18 small cardboard produce trays.

2. Duplicate each of the puppies twice. Color them.

3. Glue one puppy to the bottom of each tray.

Activity

Turn all the trays over so the puppies are facing down. Mix them up. Play concentration as you normally would. When a player makes a match, he stacks the two trays in front of him. Keep playing until all the puppies have been paired and the trays are stacked. *(Optional: When a player makes a match, everyone does the exercise.)*

EXERCISE PUPPY PATTERNS

BlueHo Bricks
38W567 Brindlewood, Elgin, Illinois 60123

113

SEQUENCE PUZZLES

Make Easy
SEQUENCE PUZZLES

1. Get 4-6 small boxes that are the same size, such as half pint milk boxes.

2. Duplicate a series of pictures such as favorite fingerplays, a short story, the growth of a flower, a bird hatching, the four seasons, getting dressed, etc. (*Start with the illustrations on these two pages.*)

3. Cut out the pictures and glue one to the side of each milk box.

Activity

Set the SEQUENCE PICTURES on a tray. Let the children put the pictures in order.

114

SEQUENCE PUZZLE PATTERNS

Buildong Blocks

38W567 Brindlewood, Elgin, Illinois 60123

RIDE AND PICK UP

(great for the gym or outside)

Activity

Spread lots of small milk cartons over the gym/outside area. Have a large box in a central location.

Have the children ride their trikes, scooters, and hoppity-hops around and pick up the boxes. When a child gets one, have her ride it over to the big box and drop it in. After all the boxes have been picked up, spread them around in different places and play again.

BOX SKATING

Activity

Have several shoe boxes and their lids. Set them on the shelf.

Let the children step into the boxes and/or lids and skate around the room. On a nice day, take the skates outside and let the children skate around the play area. *Is it easier to skate on the concrete or grass?*

HIT THE TARGET

Make the TARGET

1. Put a table about 2 feet away from an empty wall. Stand 3 or 4 shoe boxes on the table.

2. About five feet from the table, hang a long rope from your ceiling, so that it hangs about waist high. Securely tape a tennis ball to the other end of the rope.

Activity

Let a child stand behind the ball, pull it slightly back, aim it at one of the boxes, and let it go. *Did a box fall down?*

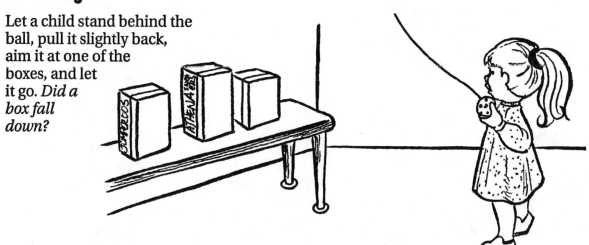

TOUCH AND TALK

Activity

Collect 5-10 small boxes *(no tops necessary)*. Cut them down so they have a 2" lip. Glue a different texture *(sandpaper, corduroy, corrugated paper, wallpaper, etc.)* in the bottom of each box. Punch a hole on one side and tie a long piece of elastic through it. Hang several texture boxes from the ceiling so they fall within arms reach of the children.

Have the children reach up, pull a box down, and feel the texture. Talk about it. Pull down another box. Discuss the differences. Rotate the boxes often to give the children different textures to TOUCH AND TALK about.

CAPTURE THE CLIPS

Activity

Pour sand in a shallow box. Mix in lots of metal paper clips. Have several magnetic wands or magnets.

Set the box, magnets, and an empty pie pan on the science table. Let the child wave the wands across the sand and CAPTURE THE CLIPS. Have them put the captured clips in the pie pan. Wave the wands again and again until all the clips have been caught.

Variation

Magnet Sort – Add other small metal objects such as washers, ball bearings, metal bingo chips, and so on. Play as above or have a sorting board for the different objects.

BIRD FEEDER

Make BIRD FEEDERS With the Children

(for each one)

1. Get a half gallon milk box. Cut out a 2"-3" square about 2" from the bottom on two opposite sides of the box.

2. Punch a hole just under the two openings. Slip a dowel rod through the holes so that it sticks out about 2" on each side of the box. *(The birds can perch on this while they eat.)*

Activity

After making bird feeder/s with your children, hang them outside so that the children can easily see them through the windows in the classroom. Each day fill the feeder/s with seed.

Throughout the day encourage the children to watch the feeders. *What is happening? Who is eating the bird seed? Are the birds perched on the dowel rods, in the feeder/s, or on the ground? Do the children think the animals like the food? How do the children know?*

Extensions

Ground Feeder – Cut down a large laundry concentrate box so it is about 2"-3" deep. Put bird seed or water in it. Set it on the ground, a log, or a large stone. Fill it each day. *Who eats and drinks from it?*

Pinecone Bird Feeder – Let the children spread peanut butter on pinecones and then roll them in bird seed. Tie a piece of twine to each one. Hang them from trees and bushes in your outside play area.

TOUCH AND FEEL

Make a TOUCH AND FEEL BOX

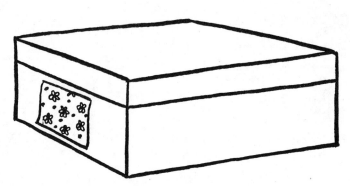

1. Get a shoe box with a lid. Cut an opening in each end of the box, just large enough for a child's hand to fit in.

2. Cut a piece of fabric a little larger than each opening. Glue the fabric to the inside of the box, so that it covers the openings.

Activity

Before the children arrive, put something in the box. Wrap a rubber band around the box to remind the children to keep the top on it. Set the box on the discovery table or window sill. Encourage the children to stick their hands in the box and feel the object. As they do, talk with them about what they are feeling. *Is is hard? Soft? Does it have points? What shape is it?* Each time they feel it, help them discover more and more about the object just by feeling it.

After several days, bring the TOUCH AND FEEL BOX to circle time. Open the BOX and see what is really in there.

Variation

Instead of Objects – Put a shallow dish in the box. Pour salt, sand, baking powder, etc. in it. Let the children feel the material. Talk about it. *What does it feel like? What do the children think it is?*

120

BUG CATCHER

Make a QUICK BUG CATCHER

1. Get a clean plastic gallon milk bottle and an old light-colored nylon stocking. Cut the top of the bottle so that it remains attached on the fourth side.

2. Cut large windows in each side of the bottle.

3. Put a little grass, a few weeds, and a stick in the bottle to make the bug feel welcome.

4. Slip the nylon over the bottle, leaving the top of the nylon open.

Activity

Take the BUG CATCHER outside. Catch bug/s. Close the top of the bottle. Loosely tie a knot in the top of the nylon. Have a magnifying glass to look at the bug/s more closely. Before going inside or when you are finished looking at the bug/s, let it go back to its natural environment.

LOAD THE FOOD TRAIN

Make the FOOD TRAIN

1. Get a box from each food group *(cereal or crackers, dried fruit, frozen vegetable, fish or meat, milk, and candy)*.

2. Connect the boxes with short pieces of colorful yarn.

3. Cut off one side of each box.

4. Cut out magazine/catalogue food pictures from each food group. Back them on construction paper and laminate or cover them with clear adhesive paper.

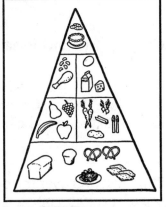

Activity

Put the FOOD TRAIN and food pictures on the science table. *(Optional: Enlarge the FOOD TRIANGLE on page 41 and tack it to the wall near the activity.)*

Let the children sort the pictures according to the appropriate categories. As the children are sorting the pictures, talk about good nutrition, balanced meals, and how food helps your body develop and grow.

EASY TERRARIUMS

You'll Need

- Clear plastic boxs with lids *(large size box used at take-out salad bars)*
- Potting soil
- Grass seed
- Water in a spray bottle

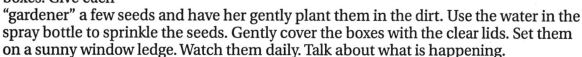

Activity

Have the children scoop dirt into the boxes. Give each "gardener" a few seeds and have her gently plant them in the dirt. Use the water in the spray bottle to sprinkle the seeds. Gently cover the boxes with the clear lids. Set them on a sunny window ledge. Watch them daily. Talk about what is happening.

Extension

Field Trip – Take a trip to a nearby greenhouse. Have one of the gardeners show the children the different plants. Talk about how it feels inside and outside the greenhouse.

DANDELION BOUQUETS

Activity

Have lots of juice boxes and a pitcher of water outside. Let the children pick dandelions and put them in their juice box "vases." Help each child pour a little water into his "vase/s."

BOX BAND

Make EASY INSTRUMENTS

- **Drums** – Punch a hole on each side of a cylinder box. Tie a long piece of colored yarn through the holes. Let the children wear them around their necks and beat them with their hands or popsicle sticks.

- **Clappers** – Get pairs of small sturdy boxes. Punch holes in two sides of each box. Loop a piece of elastic through them and tie securely. Let children slip the clappers over their hands and clap them together.

- **Bells** – Put several large bells in small sturdy boxes. Close them tightly. Let the children shake them.

- **Sand Blocks** – Glue fine sandpaper on the backsides of pairs of small sturdy boxes. Punch holes in two sides of each box. Loop a piece of elastic through them and tie securely. Let the children slip the sand blocks over their hands and rub them together.

- **Guitars** – Slip a variety of rubber bands over different boxes. Let the children strum them.

- **Shakers** – Put beans, rice, salt, sand, etc. in different small boxes. Glue them closed. Let the children shake them.

Activity

Set the instruments on the science shelf. Encourage the children to play their instruments by themselves, form large and small bands, and have classroom parades. Take opportunities to listen to the different sounds the instruments make. Talk with the musicians about making different sounds with the instruments they are playing. For example:

◆ Rub the sand blocks very slowly and softly, then very slowly but hard.

◆ Pluck the guitar rather than strum it.

◆ Flick the drum with your thumb and forefinger rather than beat it.

MATH/SCIENCE

THEME INDEX

THEME INDEX

Building Blocks

THEME INDEX

Seasons

    Fall, 15, 40, 62, 86

    Winter, 67, 119

    Spring, 25, 50-51, 119

    Summer, 73, 119, 121, 123

Self

    Physical Awareness, 52, 64, 68-69, 70-71, 76, 77, 112-113

    Self-Awareness, 19, 53, 90-91, 100, 101, 104, 106

    Self-Help, 101, 114-115

Senses

    Sight, 45, 54, 56, 72, 73, 86, 87, 107

    Touch, 44, 53, 55, 81, 83, 95, 118, 120

    Hearing, 57, 66, 76, 124-125

    Taste, 102

Shapes, 48-49, 50, 54, 55, 80, 82, 104

Sink and Float, 97

Stories, 54, 58-59, 103, 104

Teddy Bears, 95, 100

Toys, 20, 22, 44, 76, 103, 117

Vehicles, 95, 108, 116, 117, 122

Water, 85, 95, 96, 98-99

Weather, 46-47, 84, 85, 86

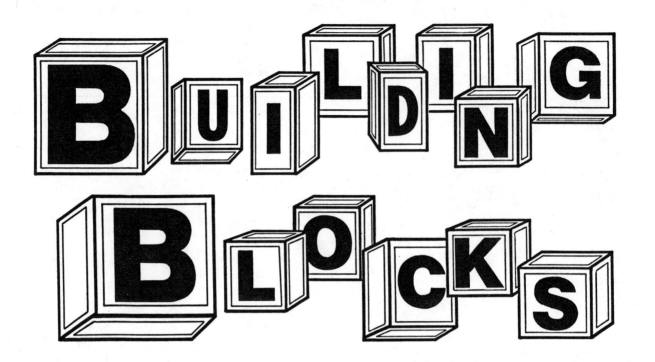

Building Blocks Library

The Circle Time Series

by Liz and Dick Wilmes. Hundreds of activities for large and small groups of children. Each book is filled with Language and Active games, Fingerplays, Songs, Stories, Snacks, and more. A great resource for every library shelf.

Circle Time Book
Captures the spirit of 39 holidays and seasons.
ISBN 0-943452-00-7   **$ 12.95**

Everyday Circle Times
Over 900 ideas. Choose from 48 topics divided into 7 sections: self-concept, basic concepts, animals, foods, science, occupations, and recreation.
ISBN 0-943452-01-5   **$16.95**

More Everyday Circle Times
Divided into the same 7 sections as EVERYDAY. Features new topics such as Birds and Pizza, plus all new ideas for some popular topics contained in EVERYDAY.
ISBN 0-943452-14-7   **$16.95**

Yearful of Circle Times
52 different topics to use weekly, by seasons, or mixed throughout the year. New Friends, Signs of Fall, Snowfolk Fun, and much more.
ISBN 0-943452-10-4   **$16.95**

Paint Without Brushes

by Liz and Dick Wilmes. Use common materials which you already have. Discover the painting possibilities in your classroom! PAINT WITHOUT BRUSHES gives your children open-ended art activities to explore paint in lots of creative ways. A valuable art resource. One you'll want to use daily.
ISBN 0-943452-15-5   **$12.95**

Gifts, Cards, and Wraps

by Wilmes and Zavodsky. Help the children sparkle with the excitement of gift giving. Filled with thoughtful gifts, unique wraps, and special cards which the children can make and give. They're sure to bring smiles.
ISBN 0-943452-06-6   **$ 7.95**

Everyday Bulletin Boards

by Wilmes and Moehling. Features borders, murals, backgrounds, and other open-ended art to display on your bulletin boards. Plus board ideas with patterns, which teachers can make and use to enhance their curriculum.
ISBN 0-943452-09-0   **$ 12.95**

Exploring Art

by Liz and Dick Wilmes. EXPLORING ART is divided by months. Over 250 art ideas for paint, chalk, doughs, scissors, and more. Easy to set-up in your classroom.
ISBN 0-943452-05-8   **$19.95**

Parachute Play

by Liz and Dick Wilmes. A year 'round approach to one of the most versatile pieces of large muscle equipment. Starting with basic techniques, PARACHUTE PLAY provides over 100 activities to use with your parachute.
ISBN 0-943452-03-1   **$ 9.95**

Classroom Parties

by Susan Spaete. Each party plan suggests decorations, trimmings, and snacks which the children can easily make to set a festive mood. Choose from games, songs, art activities, stories, and related experiences which will add to the spirit and fun.
ISBN 0-943452-07-4   **$ 8.95**

Play With Big Boxes

by Liz and Dick Wilmes. Children love big boxes. Turn them into boats, telephone booths, tents, and other play areas. Bring them to art and let children collage, build, and paint them. Use them in learning centers for games, walk-along vehicles, play stages, quiet spaces, puzzles, and more, more, more.
ISBN 0-943452-23-6   **$ 12.95**

Play With Small Boxes

by Liz and Dick Wilmes. Small boxes are free, fun, and provide unlimited possibilities. Use them for telephones, skates, scoops, pails, beds, buggies, and more. So many easy activities, you'll want to use small boxes every day.
ISBN 0-943452-24-4   **$ 12.95**

Learning Centers

by Liz and Dick Wilmes. Hundreds of open-ended activities to quickly involve and excite your children. You'll use it every time you plan and whenever you need a quick, additional activity. A must for every teacher's bookshelf.
ISBN 0-943452-13-9   **$19.95**

Felt Board Fun

by Liz and Dick Wilmes. Make your felt board come alive. Discover how versatile it is as the children become involved with a wide range of activities. This unique book has over 150 ideas with accompanying patterns.
ISBN 0-943452-02-3   **$16.95**

Table & Floor Games

by Liz and Dick Wilmes. 32 easy-to-make, fun-to-play table/floor games with accompanying patterns ready to trace or photocopy. Teach beginning concepts such as matching, counting, colors, alphabet, sorting and so on.
ISBN 0-943452-16-3   **$19.95**

Activities Unlimited

by Adler, Caton, and Cleveland. Create an enthusiasm for learning! Hundreds of innovative activities to help your children develop fine and gross motor skills, increase their language, become self-reliant, and play cooperatively. Whether you're a beginning teacher or a veteran, this book will quickly become one of your favorites.
ISBN 0-943452-17-1   **$16.95**

2's Experience Series

by Liz and Dick Wilmes. An exciting series developed especially for toddlers and twos!

2's Experience - Art
Scribble, Paint, Smear, Mix , Tear, Mold, Taste, and more. Over 150 activities, plus lots of recipes and hints.
ISBN 0-943452-21-X   **$16.95**

2's Experience - Dramatic Play
Dress up and pretend! Hundreds of imaginary characters... fire-fighters, campers, bus drivers, and more.
ISBN 0-943452-20-1   **$12.95**

2's Experience - Felt Board Fun
Make your felt board come alive. Enjoy stories, activities, and rhymes developed just for very young children. Hundreds of extra large patterns feature teddy bears, birthdays, farm animals, and much, much more.
ISBN 0-943452-19-8   **$14.95**

2's Experience - Fingerplays
A wonderful collection of easy fingerplays with accompanying games and large FINGERPLAY CARDS.
ISBN 0-943452-18-X   **$12.95**

2's Experience - Sensory Play
Hundreds of playful, multi-sensory activities to encourage children to look, listen, taste, touch, and smell.
ISBN 0-943452-22-8   **$14.95**

T O D D L E R S   &   T W O ' S